All a Novelist Needs

All a Novelist Needs

Colm Tóibín on Henry James

Colm Tóibín

Edited and with an introduction by Susan M. Griffin

The Johns Hopkins University Press

Baltimore

© 2010 The Johns Hopkins University Press
All rights reserved. Published 2010
Printed in the United States of America on acid-free paper

2 4 6 8 9 7 5 3 1

The Johns Hopkins University Press
2715 North Charles Street
Baltimore, Maryland 21218-4363
www.press.jhu.edu

Library of Congress Control Number: 2010924548

A catalog record for this book is available from the British Library.

ISBN-13: 978-0-8018-9778-8 (hardcover : alk. paper)
ISBN-10: 0-8018-9778-5 (hardcover : alk. paper)
ISBN-13: 978-0-8018-9779-5 (pbk. : alk. paper)
ISBN-10: 0-8018-9779-3 (pbk. : alk. paper)

*Special discounts are available for bulk purchases of this book.
For more information, please contact Special Sales at 410-516-6936 or
specialsales@press.jhu.edu.*

The Johns Hopkins University Press uses environmentally friendly
book materials, including recycled text paper that is composed of at least
30 percent post-consumer waste, whenever possible. All of our
book papers are acid-free, and our jackets and covers are printed on
paper with recycled content.

The last printed page of this book constitutes a continuation
of this copyright page.

CONTENTS

ACKNOWLEDGMENTS

Thanks to Kelly Blewett, Leslie Harper, and Joanne Webb for their painstaking work on the journal issue that forms the basis for this book, as well as to Jennifer Hewson for her patient help with permissions. And to Douglas for a good idea.

Susan M. Griffin

Susan M. Griffin

I have my head, thank God, full of visions. One has
never too many—one has never enough. Ah, just to
let one's self go—at last: to surrender one's self to what
through all the long years one has (quite heroically, I
think) hoped for and waited for—the mere potential, and
relative, increase of *quantity* in the material act—act of
application and production. One has prayed and hoped
and waited, in a word, to be able to work *more*. And now,
toward the end, it seems, within its limits to have come.
That is all I ask. Nothing else in the world. I bow down
to Fate, equally in submission and in gratitude. This time
it's gratitude; but the form of the gratitude, to be real and
adequate, must be large and confident action—splendid
and supreme creation. *Basta.* (*CN* 114)

Between 2002 and 2009, the accomplished fiction writer and prolific
reviewer Colm Tóibín turned often to Henry James. Across a variety of
venues—among them, the *Dublin Review*, the *Daily Telegraph*, the *Henry
James Review*, *Bookforum*, the *New York Review of Books*, Signet, Penguin,
and Folio Society editions—Tóibín published introductions, reviews,
talks, and essays on Henry James. In "A More Elaborate Web: Becoming
Henry James" (originally an address given on San Servolo in the Venetian Lagoon), Tóibín tells us his own Jamesian history: his first reading,
at nineteen, of a James novel, *The Portrait of a Lady*; his fascination with
the five-volume Leon Edel biography; the slow emergence of James as a
character for his novel; his identifications, conscious and unconscious,
with the earlier writer. *All a Novelist Needs: Colm Tóibín on Henry James*
extends and deepens that history: reading this diverse body of criticism

together, we follow Tóibín in what might best be characterized as a series
of conversations with Henry James.

Tóibín's most well-known engagement with James is his 2004 novel
The Master, which grapples with the style and substance of Henry James's
work and life. I mention Tóibín's novel at the start because the great
strength of his criticism is that he reads like a writer, joining, as he does
so, other poet-critics, including Ezra Pound, W. H. Auden, James Bald-
win, Richard Howard, and Cynthia Ozick. As this list alone illustrates,
how writers read James is a various business. What's shared is that these
are critics who write from the inside: fellow artisans who read to puzzle
out, precisely and fully, the workings of this particular novel or letter or
essay. Driven, not by program or paradigm, but by avid curiosity, and
intimately familiar with the difficulties the novelist faces, Tóibín wants to
know how and why James's writing succeeds—or fails. Reading Tóibín on
James is like reading James himself in his *Notebooks* as he worries at an
anecdote or incident: "*Plus je vais, plus je trouve* that the only balm and
the only refuge, the real solution of the pressing question of life, are in
this frequent, fruitful, intimate battle with the particular idea, with the
subject, the possibility, the place. It's the anodyne, the escape, the bound-
lessly beneficient resort. No effort in this direction is vain, no confidence
is idle, no surrender but is victorious" (*N* 84).

The Master retells a period in Henry James's life. These essays follow
suit insofar as, for Tóibín, understanding James's work demands attention to the scenes and situations of writing. This concern with biography is the very opposite of the literary criticism that James's stories so
often warn against: reading through the artist's work to discover some
hidden truth about his life. Favorably reviewing the second volume of
Sheldon Novick's biography, Tóibín compares his own reading of a James
passage with Novick's. It is, of course, the now infamous *Notebook* entry
that begins "The point for me (for fatal, for impossible expansion) is that
I knew there, *had* there, in the ghostly old C[ambridge] . . . *l'initiation
premiere*" (*CN* 319). Novick offers these words as proof that James had
sex with Oliver Wendell Holmes. Tóibín mostly disagrees: "What could
James be talking about? It seems to me that he is talking about writing,
about discovering a style and its attendant pleasures and remembering
this discovery more than forty years later as pure sensuality, in the same

way as someone not a writer might remember first love, or sexual initiation. But I am not sure" (*RB*). Characteristic here is the recognition implicit in "someone not a writer"; for Tóibín, James's reflections comprise a narrative about the writing life.

Characteristic too is the admission—even enjoyment—of uncertainty, the celebration of James's "complexity and ambiguity and secrecy" (*NY*). Tóibín maintains that "we can trace James's sometimes unwitting, unconscious, and often quite deliberate efforts to mask and explore matters that concerned him deeply and uneasily" (*NY*). We glimpse, then, not Henry James as such but what mattered to Henry James. For both writers, "the imagination is a set of haunted, half-lit rooms" (*HA*). So Tóibín lays out a detailed map of James's New York, at the same time describing the city as a "realm whose contours remain shadowy and whose topography is unresolved" (*NY*). And, although Tóibín's essay takes us through to James's last New York story, he also uses James to warn that the critic's word is not conclusion: "Nothing is my *last word* about anything—I am interminably supersubtle and analytic" (*NY*).

Nor does this collection represent Tóibín's last word on James, in the sense of either a problem solved or, one hopes, the two writers' final critical encounter. Indeed, one of the pleasures of reading Tóibín on James comes from his ability to attend differently with each approach. Such various views are, of course, the substance of Henry James's inseparable style and subject. One thinks of the dances of discovery and concealment that are both matter and method in novels like *The Wings of the Dove* and *The Golden Bowl*.

What is consistent is Tóibín's focus on the complex processes whereby James metamorphizes bits of life (anecdotes heard, figures glimpsed, experiences recalled) into art. James, Tóibín reminds us, "loved hearing half a story so that his imagination could work on the rest" (*LM*). In his essay on *The Portrait of a Lady*, Tóibín, with James, asserts a profound difference between source and story. James "believed that his novels, in all their shapeliness and formal grace, in all the nuance and shadow offered, in all their drama, were richer than life, more complete than life" (*HA*). Like others before him, Tóibín finds in the fiction traces of James's friends and family, but his interest is in the reimaginings and the permutations of these figures over the Master's career: "For a writer, the blurring of time present and time past is a way of freeing the imagination" (*NY*). Think of James's description of how he found, forgot, and rediscovered the now enriched subject of *The American*:

> I was charmed with my idea, which would take, however, much working out; and precisely because it had so much to give, I think, must I have dropped it for the time into the deep well of unconscious cerebration: not without the hope, doubtless, that it might eventually emerge from that reservoir, as one had already known the buried treasure to come to light, with a firm iridescent surface and a notable increase of weight. (*FW* 1055)

Most Jamesians know (James tells us himself) that the "germ" for "The Turn of the Screw" was a story told in passing by the Archbishop of Canterbury. Tóibín is concerned to see how this bit of gossip is woven together with other elements, known and unknown, in James's masterly ghost tale. He suggests that James's childhood experiences and present-day purchase of a country house enter into the making of the narrative: "If an aspect of Henry James himself and his siblings became both Miles and Flora, then a larger part of him became the governess" (*PE*). For Tóibín, James's attempts to gain popularity with this "pot-boiler" and to provoke a reaction in his secretary are, literally, part of the story.

The writing process that Tóibín describes—a hungry creative intelligence that takes and transforms what is needed, wherever and whenever it is found—recalls James's own description in "The Art of Fiction" of another writer's imaginative transformations:

> I remember an English novelist, a woman of genius [Anna Thackeray Ritchie], telling me that she was much commended for the impression she had managed to give in one of her tales of the nature and way of life of the French Protestant youth. She had been asked where she learned so much about this recondite being, she had been congratulated on her peculiar opportunities. These opportunities consisted in her having once, in Paris, as she ascended a staircase, passed an open door where, in the household of a *pasteur*, some of the young Protestants were seated at table round a finished meal. . . . The power to guess the unseen from the seen, to trace the implication of things, to judge the

whole piece by the pattern, the condition of feeling life in general so completely that you are well on your way to knowing any particular corner of it—this cluster of gifts may almost be said to constitute experience. (*EL* 52–53)

It is just such "experience," such power of guessing, that Tóibín shares with James. Repeatedly in these essays, we see the dovetailing of the two writers' methods. Tóibín describes a visit that he made to Lamb House while working on *The Master*. Like Anna Thackeray Ritchie glancing through an open door, Tóibín wanders with wide eyes, not knowing in advance what—if any—sight will be what James calls "workable" or "*discutable*." Lamb House provides: "I now had what I was searching for—the two objects over the mantelpieces, the view, the height of the upstairs rooms. All I needed now was to get back to work" (*HA*). Two years later, in "A More Elaborate Web," Tóibín reflects again, and more fully, on both the Master and the making of *The Master*. Although the styles are quite distinct (not least because one essay was originally given as a talk), Tóibín's reenvisioning of writing here resembles nothing so much as James's own prefaces to the New York Edition. Like James, "remounting the stream of time," Tóibín follows threads back to the various images, words, incidents, spaces, and scenes with which his fiction began. Specific as these re-creations are, Tóibín knows that the process that takes the artist from those bits of life (James calls them *données*) to the work of art itself can only be incompletely described and understood:

> the strange web that catches images and moments and prepares them to become part of a pattern, a more elaborate web, being spun in the imagination with care and precision and cunning but also being made by forces hidden from the artist, helped by the great complexity and perhaps the great white blankness of the unconscious mind, the secret self where memories are stored and where what matters looms large. (*ME*)

James was nothing if not a knowing artist, as his notebooks, critical essays, prefaces, and letters attest. He gives us (some of) what he knows went into the making of his fiction. It is the critic's job—ever inadequately, always partially—to descry the rest.

All this is not to say that Tóibín's James does not have definite attributes. "Henry James in Ireland" introduces us to James as an Irish writer. Astonishingly, for all of the early criticism on the "International Theme" and all of the recent efforts to recognize a Global James, until Tóibín, virtually no one had read Henry James with the Irish. In doing so, he recovers a James family recognized by their contemporaries. Oliver Wendell Holmes, for one, declared that to understand the Jameses, "one must remember their Irish blood" (*HI*). Delineating the family's various relations with Ireland, Tóibín does not introduce new material. But he brings disparate facts together for the first time to convincingly persuade us that Henry James's "family's intricate relationship to Ireland, which his sister embraced and he resisted, can be taken as a key to one of the locks on the vast store of his imagination, the shape and texture of his fictions" (*HI*).

And Tóibín is much interested in James among women. Lyndall Gordon's 1999 *A Private Life of Henry James: Two Women and His Art*, which focuses on James's relations with Minny Temple and Constance Fenimore Woolson, is, Tóibín claims, "the best single book that has been written about James" (*BL*). What draws him is Gordon's full, if unforgiving, exploration of "the nourishment that he [James] found not only in their [Temple's and Woolson's] lives but in their deaths" (*RB*). Certainly *A Private Life* is a book that, as Tóibín himself explains, proved useful in the writing of *The Master*, in which Temple and Woolson figure importantly. Alice Gibbens James, William's wife, has typically been either ignored or mildly mocked by Jamesians, but Tóibín finds much to admire in Susan Gunter's 2009 biography, *Alice in Jamesland*. At the same time, he more than implies that Gunter too gently glosses over Alice's meanspiritedness toward the other women in Henry's life (his sister, Edith Wharton, Theodora Bosanquet). (Tóibín can be even-handed about such things: he teases Sheldon Novick for being too "nice" to recognize how not nice Henry James could be.) Ultimately, what Tóibín cares about is the writing. He traces how James's experiences with Minny Temple and Constance Woolson, with Lizzie Boott and Clover Hooper Adams, with Alice James and Alice Gibben James, are woven into the patterns that make up his female characters. Literary women can be useful too: Tóibín, who describes James as "haunted" by George Eliot, suggests that Dorothea Brooke and Gwendolyn Harleth are summoned and exorcised in the creation of Isabel Archer. Most intriguing are the intricate, and often indirect, ways that female characters figure forth James himself: "James used everything he knew, including his complex self, when he wrote *The Portrait of a Lady*. He dramatized his own interest in freedom against his own egotism, his own bright charm against the darker areas of his imagination" (*AD*).

Tóibín gives us other Henry Jameses as well: the New Yorker, angry at his city as only a native can be; the son and brother "managing his family with slow doses of deceit" (*BL*); a morally serious James, ruthlessly selfish for his art; a homosexual James who "covered his tracks magnificently" (*RB*); a turn-of-the-century bachelor at ease with young gay men. These last Jameses are important for Tóibín, who recognizes a predecessor with whom he is not always easy. James was prominently absent as well as present in Tóibín's *Love in a Dark Time: And Other Explorations of Gay Lives and Literature* (2002). What's striking in the essays included here is that, in analyzing James's writing, Tóibín neither reads past nor stops with James's sexuality. He would like to know if James had sex with other men (most of us would), but Tóibín's own intimate relation with James is focused on apprehending how his (gay, Irish, American, solitary, social) artistic forerunner worked. Tóibín's critical project is fueled, not by an anxiety of influence, but by the need to capaciously understand.

That work of critical understanding is, as I suggested above, not wholly distinct from Tóibín's fiction writing. Starting in the 1990s, a new genre seems to have proliferated: fictions in which James appears as a central character. Versions of these Jamesian narratives have been written by, among others, Carol de Chellis (*Henry James's Midnight Song*), Kathryn Kramer (*Sweet Water*), Michiel Heyns (*The Typewriter's Tale*), Emma Tennant (*Felony*), David Lodge, (*Author, Author!*), Joyce Carol Oates ("The Master at St. Bartholomew's Hospital, 1914–1916"), Cynthia Ozick (*Dictation*), and Richard Liebmann-Smith (*The James Boys*). Varied in quality, they vary also in the depth of their engagement with James's life and work. *The Master* stands out among these, a *tour de force* of what James would call "re-vision." Tóibín describes incidents from James's life and incorporates phrases from James's writing, but what makes *The Master* Jamesian is that Colm Tóibín shares structures of imagination with Henry James.

Henry James's imagination has, of course, long been an object of fascination. Many critical works have taken up the topic: *The Imagination of Disaster* (1961) by J. A. Ward, *The Grasping Imagination* (1970) by Peter Buitenhuis, *The Melodramatic Imagination* (1976) by Peter Brooks, *The Structure of the Romantic Imagination* (1981) by Daniel Mark Fogel, *Imagination and Desire in the Novels of Henry James* (1984) by Carren Kaston, *Henry James: The Imagination of Genius* (1992) by Fred Kaplan, and *Henry James and the Imagination of Pleasure* (2002) by Tessa Hadley. I do not think it is an accident that, among these, the one that studies pleasure is written by a woman who is, like Tóibín, both critic and novelist. In his *Notebooks*, James describes again and again his deep delight in the hard work of creation: "To live *in* the world of creation—to get into it and stay in it—to frequent it and haunt it—to *think* intently and fruitfully—to woo combinations and inspirations into being by a depth and continuity of attention and meditation—this is the only thing" (*N* 62).

Is Colm Tóibín a Jamesian novelist? Such matters are not his concern. Certainly, Tóibín's most recent novel, *Brooklyn* (2009), has been read as a rewriting of James's *The Portrait of a Lady*. The affinities are there: a young woman, bright, lively, and unconventional, crosses the Atlantic in search of freedom and a richer, happier life. Once there, conventions restrict her movements even as possibilities open before her. Her old world extends into her new, bringing with it a deep distrust of happiness. The past cannot be erased or even escaped.

Yet one could never pick up *Brooklyn* and mistake it for a Henry James novel. Written in Tóibín's distinctive style, *Brooklyn* is neither pastiche nor parody nor postmodern corrective. Perhaps Tóibín himself offers us the way to describe the connection between the two writers: if Henry James was haunted by George Eliot, Colm Tóibín is haunted by Henry James. Such relations are framed by Tóibín's own words in *The Master*. He begins, "Sometimes in the night he dreamed about the dead—familiar faces and the others, half-forgotten ones, fleetingly summoned up," and ends with "the screens and the shadowed corners, and all the other rooms from whose windows he had observed the world, so that they could be remembered and captured and held."

Fittingly, then, Colm Tóibín's "Afterword" to this volume declines to sum up an argument about Henry James. Instead, Tóibín tells a story. And it is precisely a story about writing, about the specific imaginations of artists, about what stories an individual author can write and about those she does not. Perhaps most centrally, it explores what "telling" stories might mean: creative, oblique, partial, expansive, free rendering of the "facts." Fittingly as well, Tóibín suggests how this creative transmutation forges reality, not only for the writer but also for the reader and even for the one whose experience is artistically reenvisioned. James's exhortation to his fellow novelist H. G. Wells remains central: "It is art that *makes* life, makes interest, makes importance, for our consideration and application of these things, and I know of no substitute whatever for the force and beauty of its process" (*HJL* 770). Tóibín's narrative of tales told and untold imagines Lady Gregory giving Henry James a secret, but not giving herself away: "As Henry James stood up from the table, it gave her a strange sense of satisfaction that she had lodged her secret with him, a secret over-wrapped perhaps, but at least the rudiments of its shape apparent, if not to him then to her for whom these matters were pressing, urgent, and gave meaning to her life" (*A*).

What happens next is the work of other hands. Delivered to Henry James, Lady Gregory's tale about the shape of her life is put aside—he cannot use it. The gift waits, like a bundle of Venetian love letters, for the writer who will find in it, not some simple proof, but what he needs to begin:

> This is all a novelist needs, nothing exact or precise, no character to be based on an actual person, but a configuration, something distant that can be mulled over, guessed at, dreamed about, imagined, a set of shadowy relations that the writer can begin to put substance on. Changing details, adding shape, but using always something, often from years back, that had captured the imagination, or mattered somehow to the hidden self, however fleetingly or mysteriously. (*AN*)

WORKS BY COLM TÓIBÍN

A   "Afterword: Silence"
AD   "A Death, A Book, An Apartment: *The Portrait of a Lady*"

AN   "All a Novelist Needs"
BL   "A Bundle of Letters"
HA   "The Haunting of Lamb House"
HI   "Henry James in Ireland: A Footnote"
LM   "The Lessons of the Master"
ME   "A More Elaborate Web: Becoming Henry James"
NY   "Henry James's New York"
PE   "Pure Evil: 'The Turn of the Screw'"
RB   "Reflective Biography"

WORKS BY HENRY JAMES

CN   *The Complete Notebooks of Henry James*. Ed. Leon Edel and Lyall H. Powers. New York: Oxford UP, 1987.

EL   *Essays on Literature, American Writers, English Writers*. Ed. Leon Edel. New York: Library of America, 1984. Vol. 1 of *Literary Criticism*.

FW   *French Writers, Other European Writers, the Prefaces to the New York Edition*. Ed. Leon Edel. New York: Library of America, 1984. Vol. 2 of *Literary Criticism*.

HJL *Henry James Letters*. Ed. Leon Edel. Vol. 4. Cambridge: Belknap P of Harvard UP, 1984.

All a Novelist Needs

CHAPTER ONE

Henry James in Ireland

A Footnote

In 1894, two years after the death of his only sister Alice, Henry James received her diary, which had been printed in a limited edition by her friend Katherine Loring. He wrote to his brother William that he was "intensely nervous and almost sick with terror about possible publicity" arising from the diary (*HJL* 3: 479). He worried about what he called "the fearful American newspaper lying in wait for every whisper, every echo" (480). The diary was written in England while Alice was bedridden; some of the stories recounted there were told to her by Henry himself, who prided himself on his civility and discretion. When he told his sister that Augustine Birrell "has a self-satisfied smirk after he speaks," he never dreamed that she would write it down. Nonetheless, he admired her style, which he thought "heroic in its individuality" and "its beauty and eloquence" (481).

He then began to muse on his sister's politics during her eight years in England:

> The violence of her reaction against her British *ambiente*, against everything English, engenders some of her most admirable and delightful passages. . . . I find an immense eloquence in her passionate "radicalism"—her most distinguishing feature almost—which, in her, was absolutely direct and original. . . . However, what comes out in the book . . . is that she was really an Irishwoman!—transplanted, transfigured—but nonetheless fundamentally national—in spite of her so much larger and finer than Irish intelligence. She felt the Home Rule question absolutely as only an Irishwoman (not anglicised) could. It was a tremendous emotion with her—inexplicable in any other way— and perfectly explicable by "atavism." What a pity she wasn't born there—and had her health for it. She would have been . . . a national glory! (481–82)

Henry James himself had come to England in 1870, when he was twenty-seven years old, and lived in London and in Rye until his death in 1916. In the last year of his life he became a naturalized British citizen and during his last illness was conferred with the Order of Merit. He loved England and the English and suffered from neither his sister's passionate radicalism nor her atavism. Ireland, for him, represented a sort of wildness that was alien to his nature. His English friends, in general, were members of the ruling class to which Ireland presented itself as a great headache in the 1880s and 1890s, the years when Henry James dined out a great deal in London. In June 1886 he wrote to his brother about the Home Rule debate: "All the England one doesn't see may be for it—certainly the England one does is not. It seems highly probable that whatever happens here, there will be civil war in Ireland—they will stew, in a lively enough manner, in their own juice" (123).

Henry James's hostility to Ireland may have taken its bearings from his own need to distance himself from his family's close connections to the country. His grandfather William James of Albany declared his Irishness above all else in his epitaph, which read simply: "William James, A Native of Ireland, [died] December 19, 1832, aged 63" (Habegger 9). In the large memorial to him at Albany Rural Cemetery, the words "Born in Ireland" were prominently displayed. William James grew up on a twenty-five acre farm in the townland of Curkish outside Bailieborough in County Cavan, which William's older brother was to inherit. The Jameses were Presbyterians, and this meant that they were sandwiched between the local Protestant gentry of English origin and the landless Catholics. They were neither the establishment nor the illiterate poor. This class became the main Irish emigrants to America in the years before the Irish famine. Of the five thousand a year who emigrated to America in the early 1790s, for example, two-thirds came from Ulster and arrived with some capital, an education, and an interest in religious freedom and radical politics. According to family tradition, William James's first desire on crossing the Atlantic was "to visit the fields of the revolutionary battles" (11). He married Catherine Barber, two of whose uncles had been leaders in the American War of Independence. William James, as a good Irish Presbyterian, remained on the paths of righteousness all his life and attempted to ensure that his descendants should do the same. Students of Irish Presbyterian rhetoric will recognize the tone in his exhortation to his executors, to whom he gave discretionary powers to withold legacies from those who strayed:

> Although the extensive and extraordinary power herein conferred of punishing idleness and vice and of rewarding virtue, must from its nature be in a considerable degree discretionary, and although its faithful exercise may prove to be a task at once responsible and painful, yet it is my full intention and earnest wish that it shall be carried into execution with rigid impartiality, sternness and inflexibility. (qtd. in Habegger 108)

One of William James's best friends in America was the lawyer Thomas Addis Emmet, whose brother Robert Emmet led a disastrous rebellion in Dublin in 1803 and was hanged. The memory of Robert Emmet was venerated in the James family. Henry Sr., the novelist's father, could recite Emmet's speech from the dock, and Henry Jr., the novelist, referred to Emmet's memory as "a pious, indeed . . . a glorious tradition" (*AU* 25). This connection between the Jameses and the Emmets was strengthened by the marriage of two of Henry's cousins to two Emmet brothers, one of them called Robert. These two cousins were the sisters of Minny Temple, whom Henry James used as the model for Isabel Archer in *The Portrait of Lady* and Milly Theale in *The Wings of the Dove*. The house in Albany where Mrs. Touchett finds Isabel is based in detail on Catherine Barber's house in Albany where Henry James first knew Minny Temple. James remained close all his life to some of his Emmet cousins, referring to them fondly as the Emmetry.

As the nineteenth century began, William James from Bailieborough in County Cavan became immensely rich. He owned a solid block of Greenwich Village, a great deal of real estate in Syracuse, and land in Illinois. He invested in a new method of extracting salt, and it was from this and the growing city of Syracuse that he made his real fortune. He was important enough by 1825 to be chosen to give the main address when the Erie Canal arrived in Albany. When he died, the *New York Evening Post* wrote: "With the exception of Mr. Astor . . . no other business man has acquired so great a fortune in this State. To his enormous estate of three millions of dollars there are nine surviving heirs" (qtd. in *AU* 396).

William James of Bailieborough and Albany died eleven years before Henry James the novelist was born, but Henry James remembered Catherine Barber, his grandmother, well. She did not die until Henry was sixteen. In his memoir *A Small Boy and Others*, published in 1913, Henry sought to establish Catherine Barber as the ancestor to whose stock he offered greatest allegiance:

> She represented for us in our generation the only English blood—that of both her own parents—flowing in our veins; I confess that out of that association, for reasons and reasons, I feel her image most beneficently bend. . . . If I could freely have chosen moreover it was precisely from my father's mother that, fond votary of the finest faith in the vivifying and characterising force of mothers, I should have wished to borrow it; even while conscious that Catherine Barber's own people had drawn breath in American air for at least two generations before her. (*AU* 5–6)

By 1913, Henry James had become an honorary Englishman and was happy to claim some English blood. But he was mistaken, or indeed sought to mislead. His grandmother was, like himself, a great Anglophile, and she might have fooled him into thinking that her family was of English origin, but they were not. They were Irish too, being Presbyterian Scottish planters in County Longford. Thus Henry James was Irish on three sides, on the James side, on the Barber side, and on his mother's side—her grandfather Hugh Walsh came from Killyleagh in County Down in 1764. His mother's other grandfather came from Edinburgh. He did not have a single drop of English blood.

The word Irish changed its meaning between the 1830s when Henry James's millionaire grandfather could be declared "a native of Ireland" on his tombstone and the 1840s when Henry himself was growing up as the Irish poor descended on America and the word Irish became synonymous there with Catholicism and a background in dispossession. The distance between the James family and the new Irish emigrants may best be measured by the difference in attitudes toward the Civil War. Both of Henry James's younger brothers fought in the Civil War, both leading black regiments. This was the first time black soldiers had been permitted in the U.S. Army, and as Garth Wilkinson James's 54th Regiment made its way through Boston they were met with both cheers and boos but were finally attacked by an Irish mob as they neared the wharf. The James sons (and indeed the entire family) were fired with idealism and a revulsion for slavery; some of the new Irish, to say the least, were not.

The old man William James had thirteen children, none of whom followed him successfully into business. Many of them died in their twenties and thirties. His sons "turned into fashionable gentlemen who lived in idleness, or they lost their faith and turned to strange enthusiasms, or they squandered their patrimony in New York's gambling dens or on alcohol or opium" (Habegger 43). But Henry James Sr., the father of the novelist, became interested in religion and philosophy and befriended many of the great of his day, including Emerson and Thackeray. He was a free thinker, steeped in Swedenborgian visions and desperately curious to find the truth. With this end in mind, he brought his wife and five children many times across the Atlantic, concerned always about what he called their "sensuous education." His children enjoyed the joke, or at least said they did, that they did not come from any country in particular or any place. They were natives, instead, of the James family. Their Irish background and indeed their American nationality had been subsumed into a curious and creative hybrid that produced two geniuses, Henry James and his brother William.

The James family believed it had invented itself and that its eccentricities arose from an inordinate amount of foreign travel and Henry Sr.'s religious quests. But those around them believed that their strangeness was much simpler: they were Irish. Oliver Wendell Holmes, a friend and contemporary of both William and Henry, maintained that one would have to "invent a word" to describe the James household (qtd. in Gordon 32). He remembered "its keen personal intuitions, the optimistic anarchising of the old man (a spiritual, unpractical anarchism), its general go-as-you-please but demand-nothing, apotheotic Irishry." In order to understand William and Henry James, he told an English friend, "one must remember their Irish blood" (qtd. in Howe 41).

In *The Metaphysical Club: A Story of Ideas in America* Louis Menand writes: "The Jameses were not Brahmins. They were not even New Englanders. They were descended on both sides from Irish immigrants, and although the Jameses now seem as American as the Emersons and the

Holmeses, to people like the Emersons and the Holmeses they seemed rather distinctively Irish" (77). Edward Emerson, the son of the writer, left a vivid description of the James family at table, when the third brother Wilkie

> would say something and be instantly corrected or disputed by the little cock-sparrow Bob, the youngest, but good-naturedly defend his statement, and then Henry (Junior) would emerge from the silence in defence of Wilky. Then Bob would be more impertinently insistent, and Mr. James would advance as Moderator, and William, the eldest, join in. The voice of the Moderator presently would be drowned by the combatants and . . . in the excited argument, the dinner-knives might not be absent from eagerly gesticulating hands. . . . In their speech singularly mature and picturesque, as well as vehement, the Gaelic (Irish) element in their descent always showed. (James 17–18)

Henry James Sr., who due to a childhood accident walked with a wooden leg, made one visit to his father's native place, Bailieborough in County Cavan. He talked about it a great deal to his children, as Henry recounted in the second volume of his memoirs. Henry Sr. was accompanied to Cavan by his black servant Billy Taylor. "I find myself," Henry wrote, "envying the friendly youth who could bring his modest Irish kin such a fairytale from over the sea," "the representative of an American connection prodigious surely in its power to dazzle" (*AU* 396). Bailieborough consisted, the James children heard, "of the local lawyer, the doctor and the . . . principal 'merchant'" (397). The doors stood open in Bailieborough and there was whiskey on every table, and Henry Sr. met an Irish girl called Barbara, who was, according to his son, "matchlessly fair and she ate gooseberries with a charm that was in itself of the nature of a brogue" (398). The black servant Billy Taylor "singularly appealed, it was clear, to the Irish imagination, performing in a manner never to disappoint it."

The main account of this visit was recorded by Henry James in 1914. Eight years later, his nephew Harry James wrote to Robert James of Bailieborough and asked if anyone remembered the visit. Robert James replied that he had "heard of your grandfather's visit and about his negro servant," and Robert's wife "wrote that William James of Belfast . . . says he remembers well his father telling of a relative coming over with a Negro servant & all the country people standing with their mouths open, never having seen a Negro previously" (Habegger 151).

There is only one contemporary document about Henry James Sr.'s visit to Cavan in 1837, at a time when there was tension between Great Britain and the United States, and that is a brief note to his brother in his own hand:

> It would be impolitic to enlarge upon transAtlantic affairs in a docu-ment which may very probably fall into the enemy's hands, and which coming from a man of my widely acknowledged Note, might, pro-vided, of course, they should have gumption enough to decipher it, greatly aggravate the Existing embarrassments between the two coun-tries. (qtd. in Habegger 152)

The "enemy" here, jokingly referred to, does not have to be named. It was clear to the two James brothers, one in Ireland to revisit the ancestral home, that the enemy would have to be England.

Henry James's closest Irish acquaintances were Lady Gregory and her nephew Jocelyn Persse. James met Lady Gregory in 1880 in Rome while she was on her honeymoon. They both took an interest in the orphan Paul Harvey, whose aunt they had known, writing him many letters and dining together in London with him. "I often met him in London but never got very near him except on the one matter of our protecting care of Paul Harvey," Lady Gregory wrote (20n). When Paul Harvey was con-templating an unsuitable marriage, he sought advice from Henry James. Later, when Lady Gregory asked Paul what James had said, he replied: "He just said it was impossible, that I must put it out of my head" (104n). Lady Gregory commented: "The best of advice, yet we can hardly imagine one of those beings who people his pages speaking on any matter, light or serious, in such brief and decisive words." Henry James's name appears in Lady Gregory's journals as a regular guest in the 1890s ("very kind as usual" [95]; "charming and pleasant as usual" [44]). On 23 January 1894, he set down in his notebooks two anecdotes told to him by Lady Gregory. The first concerned the story of a Mrs. Marcus Lynch in County Galway, an unfaithful wife taken back by her husband with the agreement that she would be flung out once her two daughters reached a certain age. As he began to write an outline of the story in his notebook, James remarked that Lady Gregory "saw more in it than, I confess, I do" (*CN* 84), but once he had written the outline "I confess that as I roughly write it out . . . there seems to me to be more in it—in fact, its possibilities open out. . . . I see a kind of drama of the woman's hopes and fears" (85). He imagined "a rather strong short novel—80,000 to a 100,000 words" (85). The other story was about a London clergyman who discovered, at the outset of their honeymoon, a letter addressed to his wife from a former lover and decided to send her back to her parents. Thereafter he lived with her "but *never* lived with her as his wife" (86). James never worked any further on these sketches, although Lady Gregory used the first anecdote in a story that she published in 1896.

There is something strange about Lady Gregory telling James these stories two years after her husband's death. She, within a year of her marriage, had had a love affair with the poet Wilfred Scawen Blunt. She had written twelve sonnets about the liaison, which she had published under his name in a book of his poems. She had lived with her husband after the affair for ten years until his death. Her own dark concealments combined with an interest in veiled, coded disclosure. James would have understood such maneuvers, and one can imagine him watching her carefully as she told him the anecdotes. James's handling of his Irishness and his homosexuality was done using concealment, creating compartments whereby things were known to some and not to others. In his best novels, there is always a secret that, if disclosed, will be explosive; some of his greatest creations—Madame Merle, Gilbert Osmond, Kate Croy, Merton Densher, Chad Newsome, Charlotte Stant—are in possession of knowledge that is successfully concealed for most of the narrative.

In the 1890s and early years of the new century James fell in love with a number of young men, among them Jocelyn Perrse. It was, Leon Edel has written, "a case of love at first sight" (189). Perrse, who had been brought up on the family estates in County Galway, was thirty years younger than James. The letters to him are James's most explicit:

God grant accordingly that I be here when you turn up with the rich glow of travel on your manly cheek and the oaths of all the Mediterranean peoples on your your [*sic*] moustachioed lips: (as I hope, at least;

I shld. like so to hear you rip them out [)]. But I yearn, dear Jocelyn, for all your sensations & notations, & think with joy of your coming to me for a couple of days, near at hand a little later on, shaking the dew of Parnassus from your hair. (*DB* 85)

In one of his early letters, written very soon after they met, he alluded to Perrse's Irishness and, in vaguer terms, to his own:

I am no worse than usual, & I hope with all my heart . . . that your charming Irish presentiment—a real brush of the Banshee!—proving you the Celtic man of imagination like myself—doesn't mean that I'm *going* to come any sort of cropper. I shall try hard not to, for I want to hold on to *you*. (89)

Once he was established in London, it took strong emotion for James to refer to himself as a "Celtic man of imagination" to someone from his English circle of friends. It did not become a habit.

Henry James never went to Bailieborough, but he did visit Ireland three times. In 1882, on returning from America, he disembarked in Cork and traveled across the country. He wrote to a friend that Ireland had not inspired him. "Cork and Dublin," he wrote, "offered nothing abnormal save a good many constables & soldiers," adding that "[t]here was no inducement to resolve my impressions into eloquent prose" (*LL* 139). In 1891, while getting over a bout of influenza, Henry spent July and a part of August at the Royal Marine Hotel in what is now Dun Laoghaire, but was then Kingstown. He wrote two short stories there, "The Private Life" and "The Chaperon." From what he called "this disaffected shore" on July 24 he wrote to Edmund Gosse:

This place is too suburban, but a very pretty coast & sea, & I have had lovely weather and have driven the pen, which was what I wished—& also have found, what I think one doesn't always find here, convenient meat & drink. Therefore I stay 4 or 5 days more. The moment of my return to town will depend on whether I then find it feasible or not to make a little journey—of about a week—round a portion of the edge of Erin. Without it I shall go home with scarcely any Irish impressions at all—not however, I judge, that they are indispensible to life. Yet this is a really charming shore. (*EG* 79)

Henry James's third and final visit to Ireland ("an alienated isle," as he called it in a second letter to Gosse) is his best-documented and his most interesting. It shows, as if we needed demonstration, how far he had climbed on the English social ladder and how distant he genuinely felt from the Ireland his father had visited six years before his birth. The early part of 1895 was, in certain ways, the worst period of his life. He had invested huge hopes in his play *Guy Domville*, which failed in January, the author being booed off the stage. He wrote to his friend William Dean Howells: "I *have* felt, for a long time past, that I have fallen upon evil days—every sign or symbol of one's being in the least *wanted*, anywhere or by any one, having so utterly failed" (*HJL* 3: 511). His play was replaced with a new work by Oscar Wilde called *The Importance of Being Earnest*, using the same actors and the same manager. James disliked Wilde's work, despising its cheapness and facility. He was jealous of the Irishman's success in London and despondent at his own failure.

In March 1895 he came to Dublin. He stayed for the first week at Dublin Castle with the Lord Lieutenant, Lord Houghton, whose father he had also known in London. Things were not easy in Dublin; the Anglo-Irish were boycotting the season at the Castle, an event described in all its tawdriness and sadness by George Moore in his novel *A Drama in Muslin*. The Lord Lieutenant, the Queen's representative in Ireland, had to import his guests, Henry among them. Henry did not take well to being imported.

He wrote to his brother:

> My six days at the Castle were a gorgeous bore, and the little viceregal "court" a weariness alike to flesh and spirit. Young Lord Houghton, the Viceroy, "does it," as they say here very handsomely and sumptuously (having inherited just in time his uncle, Lord Crewe's, great property); but he takes himself much too seriously as a representative of royalty. . . . He means well—but he doesn't matter; and the sense of the lavish extravagance of the castle, with the beggary and squalor of Ireland at the very gates, was a most depressing, haunting discomfort. (*HJL* 4: 6)

He also wrote to his friend Theodora Sedgwick: "The six days at the Castle were a Purgatorio—I was not made for Viceregal 'Courts,' especially in countries distraught with social hatreds" (4: 8). Lord Houghton, he wrote, "is very goodlooking, rich, gentle, well-meaning, widowed [with three girls], and grabbed at; but he is too conscious a representative of royalty to be even a tolerable host; and his 'court' is moreover so deserted [he is *absolutely*, by the fine folks, boycotted] that it was grandeur terribly in the void" (9).

When Henry James's friends Lord and Lady Wolseley, Lord Wolseley being Commander of the Forces in Ireland, discovered that he was in Ireland, they pounced on him and made him come to stay with them at the Royal Hospital in Kilmainham in Dublin, which is now the Irish Museum of Modern Art. It was a great relief after the Castle, which had included not only Lord Houghton and his pomposities but, Henry wrote, "a very dull and second-rate, though large, house-party from England" (6). His stay at the Royal Hospital was, he wrote,

> a very delightful episode. . . . They *dragged* me to them, quite; but if they did so they most sweetly made it up to me. The Royal Hospital—a kind of Irish Chelsea ditto, or Invalides for 150 old Irish soldiers (founded by Charles II), is a most picturesque and stately thing. . . . It contains one of the finest great halls in the British islands, in which, on the 14th . . . Lady W. gave a remarkably beautiful fancy-ball. The ladies were each a special Gainsborough, Sir Joshua or Romney portrait, and the men (save H. J.) in uniform, court dress or (most picturesque) hunt evening dress—the prettiest of all the fopperies of the English foppish class. (6–7)

It was, he wrote, "in its pampered militarism, a very amusing *milieu* . . . for a man of peace and lover of colour" (9). But he was also concerned about the political background. He wrote: "But the *sight* of the Irish complication does nothing to make one think it less. The English are encamped there as in a foreign country—they *hold* it, for that requires no imagination. Will they ever have imagination to do more? I saw no signs of that."

This tension in James's life between his love for fopperies and color and his own heritage and deeper concerns made its way into his fiction in one story. This tale, written in 1888, is called "The Modern Warning." It tells of an American visiting Europe. Macarthy Grice does not want his sister

Agatha to marry an English M.P. The reason is that he loathes England. James enjoys pointing out the differences between Sir Rufus Chasemore, the M.P., and Mr. Grice, the American. Sir Rufus "wore old clothes which looked new, while his transatlantic brother wore new clothes which looked old" (*CS* 379). Mr. Grice is annoyed by the Englishman, being in general "much irritated by the tricks which the English played with the English language." "They have such thick hides in general that they don't notice anything," he tells his mother (383).

The dislike the American feels for the Englishman is not only about the use of language, but also about politics:

> it stuck out of the Englishman at every pore that he was a resolute and consistent conservative, a prosperous, accomplished, professional, official Tory. It gave Macarthy a kind of palpitation to think that his sister had been in danger of associating herself with such arrogant doctrines. (389)

Sir Rufus cannot understand why the American does not like him. He asks Agatha, Macarthy Grice's sister, to explain: "It's not directed to you in particular," she tells the M.P., "any dislike he may have. I have told you before that he doesn't like the English. . . . I have told you before that we are of Irish descent, on my mother's side. Her mother was a Macarthy. We have kept up the name and we have kept up the feeling" (393).

Sir Rufus replies: "I see—so that even if the Yankee were to let me off the Paddy would come down! That's a most unholy combination." Agatha tells him: "I suppose that those hostilities of race—transmitted and hereditary, as it were—are the greatest of all."

In his dramatizing of the battle between an English and American sensibility in "The Modern Warning," James portrays American democracy as open and impressive, yet his American hero, soured by his Irish background, is narrow-minded and dull, whereas the Englishman is witty and urbanely complacent. Agatha Grice is caught between the two.

James himself lived outside this conflict. He loved England, its landscape and its traditions and its people. He did not feel "the hostilities of race." As the First World War broke out he felt a strong surge of patriotic feeling. In his fiction, he made great drama between the clash of cultures, as Americans more innocent than he made their way back to the

Old World. Throughout his life, his sensibility became more refined, his tastes and indeed his prose more rarefied. In the great journey of his self-invention, he managed to erase almost completely the Irish background of which his sister was so proud, making sure that it would be a footnote to his much larger and more ambitious concerns. Thus while his American contemporaries during the years when the family lived in Newport and Boston viewed his family as Irish, no one in England viewed him as anything other than a grand American. It must have been a relief.

Throughout his life, in passing remarks, he managed a good number of throw-away, slightly disparaging remarks about Ireland. In chapter 22 of *The Portrait of a Lady*, for example, when Osmond visits his daughter Pansy in the convent, the nun informs him that they have English, German, and Irish sisters among them. Osmond, in response, "gave a smile. 'Has my daughter been under the care of one of the Irish ladies?' . . . he saw that his visitors suspected a joke, but failed to understand it" (*NO* 426). This was written in 1880. In 1906, to take another example, James wrote to Paul Harvey and bemoaned the fact that he was seeing Lady Gregory "much less than of old. She is so immersed in her Erse—I had almost said in her Hearse!" (*HJL* 4: 398). When William wanted to call his son Hagen in 1884, Henry wrote to him disapprovingly: "I don't like Hagen (it will eventually be pronounced Haygen & mistaken for the Irish Hagan)" (*WHJ* 258). In *Washington Square*, when Mrs. Pennington seeks to meet Morris Townsend, she considers where the meeting should take place. "Then she thought of the Battery, but that was rather cold and windy, besides one's being exposed to intrusion from the Irish emigrants, who at this point alight, with large appetites, in the New World" (*NO* 82).

He moved then from claiming his Celtic background to claiming English blood, from being fascinated by his sister's Irishness to erasing his own. He took a different line with many correspondents. In 1881 he wrote to his old friend Tom Perry, now teaching at Harvard: "If I had nothing else to do I think I should run over to Ireland: which may seem strange to you on the part of one satiated in his youth with the Celtic genius. The reason is that I should like to see a country in a state of revolution" (*HJL* 2: 332–34). In his letters to his old Boston friend Grace Norton he was more forthright and less amused. Ireland, he felt, could injure

England less with [Home Rule] than she does without it. . . . She seems to me an example of a country more emancipated from every bond, not only of despotism but of ordinary law, than any so-called civilized country was before—a country revelling in odious forms of irresponsibility & license. And, surely, how can one speak of the Irish as a "great people"? I see no greatness, nor any kind of superiority in them, & they seem to me an inferior & 3rd rate race, whose virtues are of the cheapest & shallowest order, while their vices are peculiarly cowardly & ferocious. They have been abominably treated in the past—but their wrongs appear, to me, in our time, to have occupied the conscience of England only too much to the exclusion of other things. (qtd. in Kaplan 294–95)

Two years later, in 1888, he wrote to her again: "Here there is nothing but Ireland, & the animosities & separations it engenders—accursed isle! Literature, art, conversation, society—everything lies dead beneath its black shadow" (296).

The figure of Parnell, however, interested him enormously: "the Satanic Parnell, who has fought like a thousand tigers & may very well *still* carry all Ireland with him; on which he will now throw himself like a tremendous firebrand." In 1889 he attended "the thrilling, throbbing Charles Stewart Parnell trial" (as did Lady Gregory and Oscar Wilde) and wrote to Grace Norton: "If one had been once and tasted blood, one was quite hungry to go again and wanted to give up everything and live there. Unfortunately, or rather, fortunately, getting in was supremely difficult." When Parnell was acquitted, he wrote:

Parnell has behaved atrociously (I mean, of course, quite outside the O'Shea case, as to which, shabby as it was, the cant is nauseous,) but he has shown extraordinary force, audacity & "cleverness." The last week has been a real drama—living, leaping & throbbing, with the acts bounding over from day to day—on a huge national stage.

In dealing with James's attitude toward Ireland as expressed in his letters to Grace Norton and, indeed, toward his homosexuality, it is important to remember that he was in both instances nonpracticing. His Presbyterian background in Ireland removed him from the fray, as it were, because the Presbyterian voice in Irish public life went underground after 1798, around the time his grandfather emigrated, and stayed there until 1912, around the time of Henry's death. To be Irish, in those years, was either to be Anglo-Irish and Church of Ireland or Catholic. The Ireland James railed against in a rhetoric worthy of his grandfather was an Ireland he had no reason, in London in the 1880s, to feel part of. All the same, an Irish Presbyterian heritage must have been hard to explain to his friends in England, and this was at the root of his attitude to Ireland.

William James, Henry's brother, took a more relaxed view of Ireland. When in 1888 Alice sent him a book called *Ireland's Disease; Notes and Impressions*, he wrote to Henry:

> Pray tell Alice I've read [it] with the greatest interest and recommended it to others. It has engendered in me a fierce desire to start of[f] the summer after next with my wife (& her if she'll join us!) and get off at Queenstown and peregrinate through the Emerald isle, keeping an eye open to the fine purchasable "sites" which will be thrown upon the market when the final *débacle* arrives! (*WHJ* 199)

William was ever the pragmatist.

William's son Harry went to Ireland in 1931 and met his cousin Helen James, who was then, according to R. W. B. Lewis in *The Jameses: A Family Narrative*, teaching music in a school in Dublin. He drove with her to Bailieborough to meet her ninety-one-year-old father Robert James. "This was the Bobby James of local fame and popularity, the grandson of William of Albany's older brother," Lewis writes (602).

> His hearing was a bit impaired and he moved with some difficulty, but he was a solicitous host and Harry liked him very much. After lunch Bobby took his American kinsman to the cemetery to see the flat tombstones carrying the names of the departed Jameses back to the first farming William: all named Robert, William, McCartney, or Jane, Harry noted. They walked over to the spot where Robert James's house had stood. The view was the same William of Albany had grown up with: the horizon line of the opposite hill a thousand yards away, and beyond it the tops of other hills making a far skyline; a scene everywhere of "green mowings, green grazings, green hedges."

"McCartney" stands out in the list of names. McCartney was the name of William James of Albany's mother, Susan, who lived until 1824. Her father was the agent for the resident of Bailieborough Castle, who collected the rent from William James. "The agent's name," according to Lewis, "was carried forward in the basic form of Cartney, first given to one of William's and Susan's many grandchildren" (4). The name remained so potent in the family that Sandy James—the grandson of William James, Henry's brother—who later retired to Glandore in County Cork, called his first child, born in the late 1940s, Cartney.

For Henry James, the naming of characters was planned with zeal. Pages of his notebooks were filled with lists of possible Christian names and surnames and names for houses. He took them from the newspapers and other such sources. He did not take them from life, from family or friends or acquaintances. So in "The Modern Warning," the use of the name Macarthy for his Irish American is unusual. In the story, the name comes from the mother's side. "[My grandmother] was a Macarthy. We have kept up the name and we kept up the feeling" (*CS* 393).

By 1888 when he wrote "The Modern Warning," James had not kept up the feeling, but the name and its resonance remained lodged in his mind. It was part of a store that he used in a few pages of his autobiography, but nowhere else. Yet his fiction is so full of silences and suppressions and erasures and things withheld that what he left out, what he did not see fit to present to the world, is a great deal more than the footnote he intended it to be. His family's intricate relationship to Ireland, which his sister embraced and he resisted, can be taken as a key to one of the locks on the vast store of his imagination, the shape and texture of his fictions.

WORKS BY HENRY JAMES

AU   *Autobiography*. Ed. Frederick W. Dupee. Princeton: Princeton UP, 1983.

CN   *The Complete Notebooks of Henry James*. Ed. Leon Edel and Lyall H. Powers. New York: Oxford UP, 1987.

CS   *Complete Stories 1884–1891*. New York: Library of America, 1999.

DB   *Dearly Beloved Friends: Henry James's Letters to Younger Men*. Ed. Susan E. Gunter and Steven H. Jobe. Ann Arbor: U of Michigan P, 2001.

EG   *Selected Letters of Henry James to Edmund Gosse 1882–1915: A Literary Friendship*. Baton Rouge: Louisiana State UP, 1988.

HJL   *Henry James Letters*. Ed. Leon Edel. 4 vols. Cambridge: Belknap P of Harvard UP, 1974–1984.

LL   *Henry James: A Life in Letters*. Ed. Philip Horne. New York: Viking, 1999.

NO   *Novels 1881–1886*. New York: Library of America, 1985.

WHJ *William and Henry James: Selected Letters*. Ed. Ignas K. Skrupskelis and Elizabeth M. Berkeley. Charlottesville: U of Virginia P, 1997.

OTHER WORKS CITED

Edel, Leon. *Henry James: The Master 1901–1916*. London: Rupert Hart-Davis, 1972.

Gordon, Lyndall. *A Private Life of Henry James: Two Women and His Art*. New York: Norton, 1998.

Gregory, Lady. *Lady Gregory's Diaries, 1892–1902*. Ed. James Pethica. New York: Oxford UP, 1996.

Habegger, Alfred. *The Father: A Life of Henry James, Sr.* New York: Farrar, 1994.

Howe, Mark DeWolfe, ed. *Holmes-Pollock Letters: The Correspondence of Mr. Justice Holmes and Sir Frederick Pollock 1874–1932*. Vol. 2. Cambridge: Harvard UP, 1941.

James, William. *Letters of William James*. Ed. Henry James. Vol. 1. Boston: Atlantic, 1920.

Kaplan, Fred. *Henry James: The Imagination of Genius*. New York: Morrow, 1992.

Lewis, R. W. B. *The Jameses: A Family Narrative*. New York: Farrar, 1991.

Menand, Louis. *The Metaphysical Club*. New York: Farrar, 2001.

CHAPTER TWO

The Haunting of Lamb House

On a bright Saturday afternoon two years ago, when I was close to completing a draft of my novel about Henry James, I went to visit Lamb House in Rye, which James leased in 1897 and bought a number of years later; he lived there until close to his death in 1916. The house, which was later inhabited by A. C. Benson, is owned by the National Trust. The downstairs rooms and the garden are open to the public on Wednesday and Saturday afternoons.

This was the house of James's dreams. He had taken holidays in the area and passed the house many times, noting the weathered brick, the sense of rich history, the stateliness without too much grandeur. He had walked the streets of Rye asking its more friendly inhabitants if there was a house for rent. The local blacksmith took James's London address, promising that he would get in touch if he heard of any suitable properties. When he wrote saying that Lamb House could be had, James rushed down to Rye to make sure of it.

The summer house where James wrote in warm weather was bombed in the war. But the walled garden is still there in all its splendor. And the house itself is full of the atmosphere of James. The modest downstairs rooms that he decorated so lovingly were furnished with advice from his friend Lady Wolseley, who believed that James had used her as the furniture-loving widow in *The Spoils of Poynton*. In the dining room the small bust of an Italian count made by Hendrik Andersen, whom James met in 1899, sits in the corner over the mantelpiece exactly where James put it when it arrived in a box from Rome. James's letters to the much younger and very handsome Andersen, which have recently been published (see Zorzi), are passionate about friendship, disappointed about Hendrik's lack of response to him, and withering about the young sculptor's overreaching ambition.

James's own ambition as a novelist was also enormous, but he understood the need for careful, slow, painstaking work, which is why he sought to leave London in his mid-fifties to find solitude in a town where there were no fashionable dinners or literary lunches.

Over the mantelpiece in the front reception room on the ground floor I found an object that took my breath away. It was a piece of needlework by James's closest friend of the 1880s, the American novelist Constance Fenimore Woolson. After her suicide in Venice in 1894, James went through her papers, burning what he did not wish the world to see, such as his own letters to her. But he must have taken this piece home with him, a way of remembering her, which he gave the same pride of place as Andersen's bust of the Italian count.

Suddenly that day, as I stood staring at Woolson's fancy work, a voice called my name. It was a London literary agent whom I knew. She was with one of her clients. She asked me what I was doing in Lamb House. I said that I was writing a book about Henry James. "So is my client," she said. She introduced me to the man who was standing beside her. "Are you writing about this house?" the agent asked. I told her that I was. As I spoke, I noticed a neatly dressed man whom I presumed was American listening to us carefully, moving closer. "Did you both say that you are writing books on James?" he asked. "Because so am I." He shook our hands cheerfully.

By this time a small crowd had gathered, marveling at the three writers pursuing the same goal. We were very careful with each other, no one wishing to say exactly how close to finishing we were. We were also very polite to each other. Then the man who rents the house from the National Trust and has the upstairs rooms as his private quarters, having heard all this, invited us to view James's old drawing room on the first floor as a special privilege. These rooms, I saw, as did my two colleagues, are grander than the one downstairs. The view of the surrounding countryside was fascinating.

I now had what I was searching for—the two objects over the mantelpieces, the view, the height of the upstairs rooms. All I needed now was to get back to work. In the meantime, I walked one last time through the downstairs rooms of Lamb House, the house where James wrote all his later masterpieces, the house where his old ghost, quiet and refined, and dedicated still perhaps to art at its most pure and life at its most complex, walks proudly now that his reputation as an artist continues to grow and his books are still being read. For me, as a novelist attempting to dramatize James's life, the five years between his failure in the theater in 1895 and his beginning to work on the three great novels, *The Wings of the Dove*, *The Ambassadors*, and *The Golden Bowl*, seemed the richest years of his life. It was a time when he looked failure straight in the eye and did not blink, but a time also when he was haunted by the deaths of his parents and his sister Alice. His moving to Lamb House in these years rescued him, offered him a haven, and, in turn, offered me, trying to imagine him, inspiration.

James was born in 1843, a year and a half after his brother William James, the psychologist. William was loud and rough; Henry bookish and nervous. From an early age Henry loved watching the world from a window. He was close to his mother, and it is eminently possible that "the obscure hurt" James spoke about in his memoirs was a conspiracy between him and his mother, who invented a disability, a strange backache, for him that allowed her favorite to stay in his room reading and granted him the freedom not to fight, as his younger brothers did, in the American Civil War.

James was close to his family and longed to get away from them. He traveled alone in his mid-twenties to Italy, having published some early stories and reviews. He lived in Rome, getting to know the American colony there, and then Paris, becoming acquainted with the great writers of the age, before moving to London and settling in England, a country he loved.

He used these cities in his work, used houses he had visited as a backdrop, and again and again used friends and family as models for his characters. His cousin Minny Temple, who died in her twenties of tuberculosis, became the eponymous Daisy Miller, Isabel Archer in *The Portrait of a Lady*, and Milly Theale in *The Wings of the Dove*; his sister Alice must have recognized herself as Rosy Muniment in *The Princess Casamassima*; Hendrik Andersen lent something to the creation of young Chad in *The Ambassadors*; Constance Fenimore Woolson became the model for Maria Gostrey in the same novel.

The reason why Henry James has survived as a novelist and why the three of us who came to Lamb House that day had been devoting years to writing about him does not come, however, from James's use of family and friends in his work, intriguing as it is. It comes from something that is almost the opposite, which was best outlined by the Master himself in a letter he wrote to his friend Grace Norton in 1880, when *The Portrait of a Lady* had appeared and Grace noticed his use of his dead cousin, Minny Temple. "You are both right and wrong about Minny Temple," James wrote.

> I had her in mind and there is in the heroine a considerable infusion of my impression of her remarkable nature. But the thing is not a portrait. Poor Minny was essentially *incomplete* and I have attempted to make my young woman more rounded, more finished. In truth everyone, in life, is incomplete, and it is [in] the work of art that in reproducing them one feels the desire to fill them out, to justify them, as it were.
> (*HJL* 2: 324)

Here, in a few sentences, was the philosophy of the novel, which made all the difference to James and makes all the difference to us now when we read him and consider his vast dedication to his art. He believed that his novels, in all their shapeliness and formal grace, in all the nuance and shadow offered, in all their drama, were richer than life, more complete than life. This does not mean he held life in contempt. Rather he longed to shape it, offer it, with his great talent and industry, significance and a sense of completion.

He was also the most tactful of artists, keeping himself and his views out of sight, always ready to disappear for the sake of his art. He did not have a dramatic life or profound opinions on matters of the day. His temperament was polite, playful, distant, steely. He was fascinated by money and by class, and by secrecy and treachery. James's own secret—his homosexuality—was well kept by the very few who knew or suspected. His dislike of Oscar Wilde arose not only from Wilde's success as a playwright in the years when James's own plays failed but from Wilde's flaunting of his sexuality and, indeed, of his Irishness.

The imagination is a set of haunted, half-lit rooms. Sometimes, we have no idea ourselves why a novel begins, why a style takes root, or a plot grows. James kept notes on work for the future, and he wrote many prefaces, some of them highly mysterious and obscure. He was self-conscious about style and form, but seldom about why certain stories fascinated him or why certain characters and situations gripped his imagination.

In the months between leasing Lamb House for the first time and actually moving there, James was immensely happy. He talked regularly to his architect; he bought furniture and pictures. He imagined his new life with relish. We have a right to feel that the fiction he wrote in those months should have been bright and happy too. But it was the opposite. In those months he wrote his most famous and most frightening story "The Turn of the Screw," which tells of a young governess arriving at a house that is fatally haunted, or else her own imagination, as she looks after two young children, is fatally diseased. Part of the story had been told to James by the Archbishop of Canterbury two years earlier and entered in his notebooks.

His governess came to this remote mansion as James was to come to Lamb House, full of innocence and expectation. James had realized, as he signed a twenty-one-year lease, that he would probably die in this house and that in turn sparked his dark imaginings and made the archbishop's story come to life. In the house, James placed a boy and a girl, natives of nowhere, abandoned children just as he and his sister Alice had felt abandoned as they moved house and continent at the whim of their father. In other words, as he prepared to move to Lamb House, James's demons became darker and more insistent, old fears and nightmares surfacing. Part of the day, he packed and made plans; the other part of the day he conjured up a most frightening scenario, using all he knew and transforming it, so that it still, more than a hundred years later, chills our blood. It makes Lamb House itself a rich and haunting site where the imagination of one of the greatest novelists in history was fired and found rest.

WORK BY HENRY JAMES

HJL   *Henry James Letters*. Ed. Leon Edel. Vol. 2. Cambridge: Belknap P of Harvard UP, 1975.

OTHER WORKS CITED

Zorzi, Rosella Mamoli, ed. *Beloved Boy: Letters to Hendrik C. Andersen, 1899–1915*. Charlottesville: U of Virginia P, 2004.

CHAPTER THREE

A More Elaborate Web

Becoming Henry James

Some years before the time I am describing, my mother changed the rooms around, the dining room to the front of the house, the sitting room to the back. She bought a new carpet for the back room, new curtains, lamps, a new fireplace, a new three-piece suite, and a first stereo. She painted the walls white and put up Impressionist prints. Her children were almost grown up; her pension, too, had slightly grown. She could afford it.

She was mainly absent that summer I came home from college, as were my siblings. I was nineteen. I should have gone to London and worked in a bar or a factory but didn't. Instead, I got a job in the local motor taxation office and spent the summer, under sporadic supervision, checking that every file was in place. It was dusty work, drudgery really, but I liked my coworkers and did not kill myself. In the evenings I came back to this strange room that had no clear, pure, direct associations with childhood. Every single object was new; only the echoes were old. Among the records there were three I listened to over and over—the first three Bach cello suites played by Janos Starker, the Beethoven Violin Concerto, and a collection of German, French, and Spanish songs sung by Victoria de los Angeles.

I began, for no special reason, to read *The Portrait of a Lady* by Henry James. I do not think I had read anything by him before, even in school. It was clear from the beginning that this was a novel of pure style, where style itself, prose style, style of dress and manners and gesture, was a sort of high morality. It was clear that Isabel Archer's innate stylishness would allow her to do justice to this rich new world to which her aunt had taken her. These ideas of style were not current in Ireland at the time, and I found them deeply interesting and absorbing.

Thus I was not prepared for the plot of the book, which I found shocking, not only for itself, but because the idea of style as morality, so perfectly set up, had been so summarily shattered. James as dramatist had decided that his conflict should not be between style and failure of style but between right and wrong, truth and lies, deception and honesty. I had misunderstood everything and that realization, as well as the drama surrounding duplicity, seemed to give me pleasure.

In the meantime, Victoria de los Angeles seemed to win out over Bach and Beethoven. There was a great yearning in her voice, a grace of expression mixed with acknowledged pain. Slowly, I began to associate these songs by Schubert and Debussy and Falla with Isabel Archer. I looked forward to coming home every evening to this back room and these two women who wanted something rich from life that life was slowly denying them.

I never once thought about Henry James himself. He seemed beautifully absent from his own novel, which was another aspect of his power. Over the next few years I read all of his novels and some of his stories. I could not find him in his books, and this was strangely more satisfying than finding James Joyce's life and his city all over his books, or George Eliot's opinions all over hers.

More than twenty years later, I had to review *A History of Gay Literature* by Gregory Woods for the *London Review of Books*. James loomed large in this. I was concerned about the argument that his novels were merely a way of disclosing or concealing his homosexuality. I went and read about his life in Leon Edel's biography. Some time later, at Yaddo, the artists' retreat in upstate New York, I found another set of Edel's five-volume biography of James. I took it to my room, believing that reading it from beginning to end might keep me busy and bore me at the same time, might occupy me without disturbing me so I could get on with finishing my novel *The Blackwater Lightship*. It was, of course, fascinating.

Over the next year I began to imagine James. He came to me as the protagonist of my novel *The Heather Blazing* had come—a distant, refined, mostly silent figure, middle-aged, haunted by flickering figures from the past, animated mostly by work. The life of the novel that slowly grew in my dreams would be the life of his mind.

In my six novels, I have worked only with one main character, one interior life, one intimacy. I could not imagine writing a novel with two main characters. Maybe this was what mattered to me so much when I read James first, his use of the third person intimate, his gathering of detail after detail all observed and experienced by one character, mediated by one consciousness until that consciousness slowly works on the reader until the reader becomes, or half-becomes, or almost becomes, that central consciousness. This character comes to me slowly and gradually, over a year maybe, or more. It soaks itself into my imagination. But the structure and plot do not come in this way. They can come in a flash or not come at all. I never take notes. If something cannot be remembered, then it is not important.

Waiting for a character to emerge is lazy work. You can go to the Himalayas and dream him or her up, you can stay in bed, go for a walk. All of this is work, and it would be easy to feel that you could continue like this for years and the book would somehow not only imagine itself, but write itself. But there comes a time in the imagining process when you must pounce. Early in the year 2000 I decided it was time to pounce. I had arranged, in any case, to go to the Santa Maddalena Foundation outside Florence, but I knew now that I was going to begin the novel there close to places that James had known and loved. When Beatrice Rezzoni, my hostess, asked me before I arrived if there was anything special I would need, I said yes, I, as a boy from a provincial town in Ireland, was in urgent need of meeting some posh people. That, I was told, could easily be arranged.

It was strange, despite the wars, how much the idea of society, an intact aristocracy, had survived in Italy. Many of them came to the house. They believed in ideas of good families, they believed in old money and spoke with equal awe about newly acquired wealth. Some days I wandered in Florence, looking at pictures, visiting churches. I was in my mid-forties, bald, unattached, bookish. I liked company and I liked being alone. This meant that the house at Santa Maddalena worked wonders for me. There was company for lunch and supper, but my own quarters were sacrosanct. I was meant to be working and could not be disturbed. I loved closing my door.

I worked first on a short story set in provincial Ireland, but I knew this was a form of idling, that I would have to start the book, which had formed in my head as beginning in January 1895 and ending on New

Year's Eve 1899. The working title was *The Turn of the Century.* So I wrote down "Chapter One: January 1895." Then I idled once more, went into Florence, looked at the Masaccios and worked on my short story.

One day I decided that no matter what happened it would become the opening of my novel. Anything that day would be made into drama. The sun rose and made its way across the sky as far as I could see, and then it grew dark. That could be an opening. I had my breakfast, I dreamed, I idled, I ate more, I slept. That might be enough. When my fellow guest announced that he was going to Siena, I announced that I was going with him. He knew the city, and I did not. We left too late. It was dark when we arrived. He wanted to walk up to the main square, the famous Campo. We were on a side street, lit by lamps in the wall. There were shops and cafés and restaurants. We were in a hurry, needing to get to a museum or a church before it closed at a certain time, six or seven. He was suggesting that we hurry. There were people on the street, students maybe, half blocking our way and we had to push past them. I wanted to go into the square by the first available entrance but my friend said no. He insisted that we should walk up further, to enter the square by the most perfect route. It was very beautiful when we entered, like something from a painting, and there were figures in the middle of the square and they were, I think, workers and there was some sort of demonstration and one or two of them turned towards us but for no special reason. Our museum was closed but we looked at a few churches and then we went home. I had my opening. The scene became the first pages of my book.

The next day as I worked, a piece of video art by Bill Viola, which I had looked at very closely when it showed in Dublin, came into my mind. It was of three figures of women in an Italian square and they were seeking something, or beseeching someone for something. Slowly, they made their way into the scene as well.

Soon, with the first scene nearly finished, the second scene came. Helen Volkonsky, the Princess Volkonsky, came to lunch. She was the granddaughter of Tolstoy's Prince Bolkonsky and also Stolypin, the Russian reformer. She had been born in Italy and was now, in a changed political climate, about to go to Russia for the first time. I studied her closely and soon I was back in my room working out a way of having her visit Henry James in January 1895, bringing with her a whiff of his years in

Paris and a sense of a worldliness and a cosmopolitan, almost decadent, life that he seemed to have abandoned in London, despite his social success. My Princess, of course, had nothing to do with the real visitor, who was a most respectable person, but it stirred an image that I then used.

In those days I was also reading books by and about James, and I had beside the bed one of the most useful books on Henry James, called *The Legend of the Master*, edited by Simon Nowell-Smith, published in 1948. This consists of quotes about James taken from books by his friends and family. On page 119 of that book there is an extraordinary passage from Edmund Gosse, with a note to say that James had told Hugh Walpole the same story. Gosse was staying with James in Rye and, on going for a walk with him, found that the Master was

> in profuse and enigmatic language . . . recounting to me an experience. . . . He spoke of standing on the pavement of a city, in the dusk, and of gazing upwards across the misty street, watching, watching for the lighting of a lamp in a window on the third storey. And the lamp blazed out, and through bursting tears he strained to see what was behind it, the unapproachable face. And for hours he stood there, wet with the rain, brushed by the phantom hurrying figures of the scene, and never from behind the lamp was for one moment visible the face.

Gosse then wrote:

> The mysterious and poignant revelation closed, and one could make no comment, ask no question, being throttled oneself by an overpowering emotion. And for a long time Henry James shuffled beside me in the darkness, shaking the dew off the laurels, and still there was no sound at all in the garden but what our heels made crunching the gravel, nor was the silence broken when suddenly we entered the house and he disappeared for an hour.

It is as difficult for the reader to find echoes of this passage in the work of James as it is difficult to make any direct connections between a sound and the echoes, which may be, in fact, echoes of another sound. Yet there is a story from 1878, one of James's very worst stories, and that is, in my opinion, saying a great deal, for he wrote some very bad stories. The

story is called "Rose-Agathe," and it is set in Paris and begins as a man
from a window watches a woman in the street, noting her beauty. He then
watches a male friend stand in the same street watching, he supposes, the
same woman through the window of her husband's hairdresser's shop. All
the time our narrator is at his Parisian window studying the scene below,
even as "the lamps were lighted in the hairdresser's shop."

The other scene involving a window in Paris with an observer and
an observed is one of James's most moving dramatic moments. It is in
Book Two of *The Ambassadors* when Strether comes to the street where
he knows that Chad lives: "Two or three of the windows stood open to
the violet air; and, before Strether had cut the knot by crossing, a young
man had come out and looked about him, had lighted a cigarette and
tossed the match over, and then, resting on the rail, had given himself up
to watching the life below while he smoked" (*AB* 69).

The Princess in my first chapter reminds James and the reader of an
earlier life, one of easy duplicity; she reminds him too of a resonant name
and a resonant moment, which he wishes briefly to set down on paper
and then destroy and conceal for ever. James is my character and I want
him haunted, uneasy but charming; I want his sexuality to be concealed,
unspoken, with no private sexual moments shared with the reader—the
reader must be like the wider world, kept at arm's length. This is the nineteenth century. This is a reticent man from a Puritan place, ready to do
battle on behalf of freedom for his characters, but more skilled at allowing them to renounce what freedom might come their way for the sake of
other things that are harder to define.

These scenes, so aleatory in their origin, were merely preparations for
the larger drama of the first chapter of my book, which was the failure of
Henry James's play *Guy Domville* on the London stage in January 1895.
These few months offered a drama that any novelist would work with.
The failure of James's play, the replacement, using the same theater and
the same producer, by the first production of *The Importance of Being
Earnest*. James's attending of another Wilde play, *An Ideal Husband*, on
his own opening night. Wilde's two successful plays on the London stage
helping Wilde to believe that he was invulnerable. James, within days of
his own failure, getting the story that became "The Turn of the Screw"

from the Archbishop of Canterbury. James going to Ireland, staying one week each with the Lord Lieutenant and the Commander of her Majesty's Forces. Then the Wilde trials.

Thus I had the opening of the book, and the intensity with which I could handle James's failure in the theater might have been greatly assisted by an event that occurred to me four months before I began to write the opening chapter of the book, although I did not realize this until later. In September 1999, my previous novel *The Blackwater Lightship* was short-listed, with five other books, for the Booker Prize. There is an interval of some weeks between the announcement of the short list and the announcement of the winner. This last event is done at a long, long dinner in London where many happy people eat a huge dinner and guzzle great quantities of wine and champagne. No one knows as we eat our dinners who has won. The six short-listed authors try and eat too, but it is easier to drink and it would, if drugs were available, be easier to take drugs. At some point towards the end of the dinner the five judges march into the hall; they are a cross between a pared-down jury and a horde of desperately willing executioners. For weeks you have been waiting for this moment, what James called "the enraptured moment" when finally your talent is recognized, when your book will become, as it richly deserves, a best-seller all over the world. In order to increase your hope and expectation, there are six cameras and sets of lights in the vast ballroom, one camera is focused on each author. It seems as though each of us have won. There is much fanfare and a long speech. And then the cameras come closer, right into your face, as the name is about to be read out. It is time. You are ready, despite the vast quantity of wine and champagne you have been drinking. Sudden fame, a speech to the world, cameras, lights, and much applause are a great way of making you sober. And then the name is read out and it is not yours. Within an instant, the lights are turned off and the cameras packed up and no one is looking at you. You feel a strange guilt and shame. You wish you were at home. Alone. But now you have to brave the night, speak to your publishers, accept commiserations, smile. You are an outsider in London and you wish you were sitting in lamplight with a fire lighting and the servants all asleep, and you leafing through Flaubert's letters.

Instead you will have to do what James did in my novel when his play failed: "He could not give in to his own horrible urge to be alone in the darkness, to escape into the night and walk as though he had written nothing and was nobody. He would have to go to them and thank them. . . . In the half light he stood preparing himself, steeling himself, ready to suppress whatever his own urges and needs might be" (18). I wrote that section without realizing that the Booker experience was still raw, still preying on my mind. I do not know whether the many accounts of that evening in London in January 1895, including James's letters describing his anguish and his humiliation and his determination to recover, or my own experience in London a few months before mattered more to me as I composed the first chapter of my novel.

Over the months that followed I went to look at some places in Italy associated with James. I thought it was astonishing that his friends Constance Fenimore Woolson, John Addington Symonds, and William Wetmore Story were buried so close to each other in the English cemetery in Rome where James had buried Daisy Miller years earlier. I stood in front of those graves as he must have done. Once, it was a beautiful June morning, and the place had an aura of beauty and peace. I remember feeling something I had never felt before: death as a sort of completion. I stood by Keats's grave and let the feeling sink in, and I wondered if I could put that into the novel somewhere, allow my character to have that feeling on such a morning in this place. Around this time, too, I read two books that made me feel that I should stop writing now that I had the first chapter done and keep thinking, imagining, and planning. One was Lyndall Gordon's book *A Private Life*, about Henry James's relationship to his cousin Minny Temple and his friend Constance Fenimore Woolson; the other was a book called *Amato Ragazzo*, edited by Rosella Mamoli Zorzi, the letters of Henry James to Hendrik Andersen, which I bought in Rome at the Museum near Piazza di Populo, dedicated to the work of Hendrik Andersen, where my book, in its Italian edition, would be launched in 2004.

As I walked in Venice, or in the area around Piazza di Spagna and Via Margutta in Rome, which was lovely work and sure beat looking into my own heart or walking around rainy Irish provincial towns, I became uneasy about Lyndall Gordon's version of James as I had a number of years earlier about those who tried to explain James's artistry and his genius as a form of neurosis arising from his homosexuality. I realized slowly that her blaming of James offered me a great subject that I could dramatize ambiguously, without judgment, building up detail but making no comment. James, here, could be both good and bad to the extent that neither of those words could mean anything. This, I knew, would require some care because the reader's first instinct is to judge. I knew that all of my novel, every single thing observed and understood, would be seen through James's eyes. Lyndall Gordon had seen things through the eyes of Minny Temple and Constance Fenimore Woolson, who were the innocent parties. But what if James were innocent too, or if such a term could also be rendered meaningless by the careful application of slow detail?

In September 2001 I began to work in earnest on the novel. I had nothing else to do. Each day I would take down the books I needed. Since I was writing the Alice chapter, which was to be chapter 2 (and later became chapter 3), I had her diary and her letters and Jean Strouse's biography beside me, as well as a copy of *The Bostonians* and *The Princess Casamassima* in case I needed them. But I needed, more than anything, just to start. Once I had asked a painter how to start a painting and he said: "Just make a mark." I was working in longhand in a notebook, leaving the left hand page blank for corrections. So I just made a mark.

It is, I think, possible to exaggerate the amount of the secret self that goes into any book. Sometimes, I hope, you can work on a surface level, inventing if you need to invent, using given material if the novel is about a set of events that have been already charted, or imagined material otherwise. By the end of *The Master* I simply did not know if certain moments of the book took their bearings from things that were important for me or were merely inventions, images made to satisfy the pattern I was making in the book, or images made in my own likeness. In the time I was writing the chapter on James and Oscar Wilde, I was hearing stories about priests whom I had known personally going to court for sexual abuse of minors. A few days I was like James himself, sitting at home writing a book, waiting curiously for a phone call to keep me informed about the case against Father X. But maybe this had nothing to do with the Wilde chapter; maybe the book needed such a chapter, whether I needed to tell the story or not. So, too, in those months, I was involved in the plight of two children, or rather young adults whom I had known as children, and was deeply alert to the problems and dangers facing them, and that they had faced. I think it is impossible that some of this did not make its way into the creation throughout the first half of the book of images of children in danger, children left alone, which become the young girl Mona in Ireland, who is an invention, or Henry James and his sister Alice, or Henry and William, or Miles and Flora in "The Turn of the Screw," or the two sons of Oscar Wilde. I knew I was patterning as I dramatized these pairs of children, but whether the underlying impulse to pattern so densely was entirely artistic I do not know.

The days passed. I was working, typing each chapter as it was finished, making changes between the holograph manuscript and the typed version. I read some James or something about James every day.

I was interested in placing a set of images throughout the book of what I should call sexual almostness. Hammond the servant in Ireland is invented, one of the few fully invented characters in the book, for that purpose. The scene I outlined earlier in the street in Paris staring up at a window is another. The naked figure of Gus Barker; the scene in bed with Oliver Wendell Holmes; the arrival in Rye of Hendrik Andersen. I found myself hungrily watching out for more such images I could use. One day I was idly rereading Sheldon M. Novick's book *Henry James: The Young Master* when I came across an astonishing sentence at the very end of chapter 3 about the Jameses' sojourn at Boulogne sur Mer: "When Father was at home, Harry sometimes joined him on walks, as he had done long ago in New York; and one afternoon they walked near the beach, Father talking as usual, his eyes following a young fisherwoman as with fine stride and shining limbs she waded from the sea with her basketful of glistering black shrimps" (58). The footnote for this tells us that it was a letter Henry James Senior wrote to Anne Ward on 2 November 1857, which is in the Houghton Library. It is unpublished.

I knew, as I worked on the opening of chapter 5, which was going to deal with sexual desire in all its almostness, with Gray and Holmes and Minny Temple, with Holmes and Henry James, I knew what I could do with that one sentence. This is the passage I produced in response to it:

> In the time they lived in Boulogne, Henry walked with his father on the beach. On one of those occasions, it was a windless and calm day,

the beginning of summer, with a long sandy expanse and a wide sweep of sea. They had been to a café with large clear windows and a floor sprinkled with bran in a manner that gave it for Henry something of the charm of the circus. It was empty save for an old gentleman who picked his teeth with great facial contortions and another gentleman who soaked his buttered rolls in his coffee, to Henry's fascinated pleasure, and then disposed of them in the little interval between his nose and his chin. Henry did not wish to leave, but his father wanted his daily walk on the beach and thus he had to abandon his delight in observing the eating habits of the French.

His father must have talked as they went along. The image in his mind now, in any case, was of his gesticulating, discussing a lecture or a book or a new set of ideas. He liked his father talking, especially when William was elsewhere.

They did not paddle or walk too near the waves. His memory was that they walked briskly. His father may even have carried a stick. It was a picture of happiness. And for a stranger watching, it might have remained like that, an idyllic scene of a father and son at ease together in the late morning on the beach in Boulogne. There was a woman bathing, a young woman being watched by an older woman on the beach. The bather was large, perhaps even overweight, and well protected from the elements by an elaborate costume. She swam out expertly, allowing herself to float back with the waves. Then she stood facing out to sea letting her hands play with the water. Henry barely noticed her at first as his father stopped and made as though to examine something on the far horizon. Then his father walked forward for a while, silently, distracted, and turned back to study the horizon once more. This time Henry realized that he was watching the bather, examining her fiercely and hungrily and then turning away, observing the low dunes behind him, pretending that they also interested him to the same intense degree.

As his father turned away once more and began walking towards home, he sounded out of breath and did not speak. Henry wanted to find an excuse to run ahead and get away from him, but then his father turned again, the expression on his face vivid, the skin blotched and the eyes sharp as though he were angry. His father was now standing on the shore, trembling, watching the swimmer who had her back to him, her costume clinging to her. His father made no further effort to seem casual. His stare was deliberate and pointed, but no one else noticed it. The woman did not look behind, and her companion had moved away. It was important, Henry knew, for him to pretend that this was nothing; there was no question that this could be mentioned or commented on. His father did not move, and seemed unaware of his presence, but he must have known he was there, Henry thought, and whatever this was, this keen-eyed drinking in of the woman bather, it was enough to make his father not care about Henry's presence. Finally, as he turned and set out on the journey home, his father stared back regularly with the look of someone who had been hunted down and defeated. The woman, once more, swam out to sea. (80–81)

Alert readers will know that before I began to write, I crossed the room and searched for a book. It was, of course, *What Maisie Knew*, which has a long sequence set in Boulogne sur Mer. I needed something to anchor this passage I was writing, to make a bridge between James's experience and his work, as the book I was writing was a bridge between my experience and James's work. What I needed were the opening thirteen lines of chapter 30 of *What Maisie Knew*:

> After they were seated there it was different: the place was not below the hotel, but further along the quay; with wide, clear windows and a floor sprinkled with bran in a manner that gave it for Maisie something of the added charm of a circus. They had pretty much to themselves the painted spaces and the red plush benches; these were shared by a few scattered gentlemen who picked teeth, with facial contortions, behind little bare tables, and by an old personage in particular, a very old personage with a red ribbon in his buttonhole, whose manner of soaking buttered rolls in coffee and then disposing of them in the little that was left of the interval between his nose and chin might at a less anxious hour have cast upon Maisie an almost envious spell. (622)

This was a way of anchoring my images and phrases in those of James, by riffing on them, referring to them, stealing them.

The image of his father on the beach in Boulogne was recorded not only by the father himself, but it remained in Henry James Junior's mind for forty years. He used it in *What Maisie Knew* when he came to the scenes set in Boulogne. In chapter 22, Sir Claude "with a kind of absent gaze . . . followed the fine stride and shining limbs of a young fishwife who had just waded out of the sea with her basketful of shrimps. His thought came back to her [Maisie] sooner than his eyes" (562).

In other words, an event in 1857, a tiny moment by the sea, is remembered and used by Henry James forty years later in a novel. We know the event occurred by a stray reference in a contemporary letter. We presume that James's novels are peppered with such raids on the real as a way of anchoring them in time, as a way of restoring what is lost to the publicity of the printed page. We will never be able to know which of his images were from memory and which from imagination. But the scene in Boulogne and its rendering in a novel make clear, in any case, that personal experience for James, as for most novelists, was the bank from which some of his images were borrowed.

I am pointing this out—much of it is obvious—merely to show that my own method of merging the deeply personal with the imagined, matters that come deliberately and also unwillingly and unconsciously, belongs to the main method by which novelists work and by which James himself, the supreme novelist, also worked. It allows for Freudian reading of novels and for novels to be read as a form of neurosis, but it is often much simpler: things that have mattered emotionally, often for the quality of their pattern, their beauty, their emotional shape, things that are not necessarily traumatic, lodge in the mind, becoming shadows until you sit at a desk and begin to work out a pattern of words and images and then they become substantial and they block the way of narrative progress until they are allowed onto the page, or they offer the narrative great body and substance until they become the secret subject of the book.

The importance of the five years I chose is not that Henry James had a failure in the theater, or not that he moved to Rye, or not that he wrote "The Turn of the Screw," or not that he began to dictate his fiction, although all of these things are of interest and can be dramatized. The importance of the years 1895 to 1900 is that Henry James was building up the images and figures that would constitute the three masterpieces he was gathering all his strength to write: *The Ambassadors*, *The Wings of the Dove, The Golden Bowl.* As I worked, I was acutely alert to the idea that small moments, recurring memories, a sudden realization, something half understood, random matters, all of these can make their way into the foreground or background of a novel. As you are working on one book, material can occur to you that you will not use for years, you may not plan to use it, or realize its significance—and in James's notebooks, a novel often appears as a very small idea for a short story, or just the name of a character—and the more intensely you are working, the more easily these images will come.

In my book, I offer him some of the images he will need for his last great novel, *The Golden Bowl.* The antique dealer in my book, whom the fictional James sees in 1897, will soon be his antique dealer in *The Golden Bowl.* The whiff of sexual secrecy and intrigue in the antique shop in my book will soon be part of the strange web that catches images and moments and prepares them to become part of a pattern, a more elaborate web, being spun in the imagination with care and precision and cunning but also being made by forces hidden from the artist, helped by the great complexity and perhaps the great white blankness of the unconscious mind, the secret self where memories are stored and where what matters looms large.

WORKS BY HENRY JAMES

AM   *The Ambassadors.* New York: Norton, 1964.
 What Maisie Knew. Novels, 1896–1899. New York: Library of America, 2003.

OTHER WORKS CITED

Novick, Sheldon M. *Henry James: The Young Master.* New York: Random, 1996.
Nowell-Smith, Simon. *The Legend of the Master.* New York: Scribner's, 1948.
Tóibín, Colm. *The Master.* New York: Scribner, 2004.

CHAPTER FOUR

Pure Evil

"The Turn of the Screw"

In January 1895, when Henry James was in the depths of depression due to the failure of *Guy Domville*, the Archbishop of Canterbury told him the story that became "The Turn of the Screw." James wrote in his notebook:

> Note here the ghost-story told me at Addington (evening of Thursday 10th), by the Archbishop of Canterbury . . . the story of the young children . . . left to the care of servants in an old country-house, through the death, presumably, of parents. The servants, wicked and depraved, corrupt and deprave the children. . . . The servants *die* (the story vague about the way of it) and their apparitions, figures, return to haunt the house *and* children, to whom they seem to beckon. . . . It is all obscure and imperfect, the picture, the story, but there is a suggestion of strangely gruesome effect in it. The story to be told . . . by an outside spectator, observer. (*CN* 109)

James let the story ferment in his mind for more than two and a half years before he set to work on it. Although for most of his career he was sadly aware that his books would never attract a large audience, there were times when he directly and openly sought popularity. The year 1897, when James took up again the Archbishop's story, was one of them. Through his friend William Dean Howells he had made contact with a new young editor at *Collier's Magazine* in the United States, to whom he sold the serial rights for his new fiction. He deliberately made "The Turn of the Screw" as frightening and dramatic as he could because he needed a new audience in America. So frightening, indeed, that he actually frightened himself. When he came to correct the proofs of the story, which was serialized over twelve issues in 1898, he told his friend Edmund Gosse: "When I had finished them I was so frightened that I was afraid to go upstairs to bed" (Gosse 38).

The story, on publication, caused strong reaction. The *New York Tribune* called it "one of the most thrilling stories we have ever read" (*TS* 151); the *Outlook* called it "distinctly repulsive"; the *Bookman* "cruel and untrue" (153); the *Independent* "the most hopelessly evil story that we have ever read in any literature" (156). The *American Monthly Review of Reviews* called it "the finest work he has ever done. . . . a beautiful pearl: something perfect, rounded, calm, unforgettable" (155). *Ainslee's Magazine*, however, warned its readers in December 1898 that Henry James "is by no means a safe author to give for a Christmas gift" (154).

The story has had enormous influence: indirectly, for example, on the structure and tone of Joseph Conrad's *Heart of Darkness*, begun very soon after Conrad read "The Turn of the Screw," and on films such as *The Others*, made in 2001, starring Nicole Kidman. In 1954 Benjamin Britten's opera based on the story was first produced. In 1971, Marlon Brando starred as the evil Peter Quint in *The Nightcomers*, a dark prequel to James's story. In 1974 ABC Television in the United States made a rather clunky version of the story with Lynn Redgrave as the governess. But it is the 1961 adaptation, called *The Innocents*—scripted by William Archibald, who wrote the Broadway play of the story, and Truman Capote, with some dialogue by John Mortimer, and starring Deborah Kerr—that best catches the psychological eeriness, the claustrophobia, and the essential ambiguity of the original story by James.

James loved hearing half a story, which was what the Archbishop of Canterbury told him on 10 January 1895. He then could fill in the rest. "I wrought it into a fantastic fiction," he wrote to A. C. Benson, the Archbishop's son, when the story was finished (*LHJ* 279). To begin with, he framed the story. A man at a country house party sends home for a long-locked-up manuscript to amuse and horrify his companions. In this manuscript the story of the children—a boy and a girl—and the dead, corrupt, haunting servants is recounted, in the first person, by the new governess arriving at a remote house where the children are unprotected.

For even the laziest reader of "The Turn of the Screw," the governess's tone appears overwrought and her attitude self-regarding. Soon, however, in the light of what she begins to see and sense, this ceases to matter. There are phrases and scenes in the book written with such skill and care and trickery as to make any reader follow it with a great unease. James was right to be frightened. It is a very frightening story.

James told H. G. Wells that "The Turn of the Screw" was "essentially a pot-boiler" (*HJL* 86), repeating the phrase ten days later to another correspondent, calling it "a shameless pot-boiler" (88). The word "pot-boiler" might seem a way for James to describe something less than holy, less than worthy, below the high line to which he wanted his art to ascend. But in a letter to Hendrik Andersen, written eight years later, he used the word "pot-boiler" to mean, as he explains, something "which represents, in the lives of all artists, some of the most beautiful things ever done by them" (*BB* 75). He was never simple, Henry James.

This lack of simplicity is what gives "The Turn of the Screw" its power. It is, on one level, a deeply and perhaps unconsciously autobiographical story. Because of their restless father, the James children had no peer group or set of close friends as they were growing up. They were looked after a great deal by their Aunt Kate. It would not have been hard for Henry James to imagine an adolescent boy with no friends who broke rules—his brother William was like that—or a strangely wilful unprotected girl—his invalid sister Alice, who arrived in England in 1884 to be near him, was like that.

If an aspect of Henry James himself and his siblings became both Miles and Flora, then a larger part of him became the governess. Composing the story in London while repairs were being done on his first house, imagining with friends and correspondents what it was going to be like to travel alone to live in a home with a history. He was, like his creation, thrilled and frightened at the prospect.

By the time he composed "The Turn of the Screw," Henry James had ceased to write in longhand and begun to dictate his stories and novels to a secretary. His first "typewriter" was a dour Scot called MacAlpine. He told a friend how he had meant "to scare the whole world with that story; . . . Judge of my dismay when from first to last page this iron Scot betrayed not the slightest shade of feeling! I dictated to him sentences that I thought would make him leap from his chair; he short-handed them as though they had been geometry" (Phelps 324).

In the twentieth century, the critics, led by Edmund Wilson, got to work on the story with the same cold attitude as the Scottish amanuensis. The ghosts, it was pointed out, were never actually seen by the children or by the housekeeper in the story but by the governess alone. The ghosts, it was suggested, were aspects of the deep neurosis that affected our hysterical governess. Rather than a ghost story, Wilson concluded in 1934, "The Turn of the Screw" was "a study in morbid psychology" (*TS* 172). The American poet and critic Allen Tate in 1942 supported Wilson: "James knew substantially all that Freud knew before Freud came on the scene" (*TS* 176).

The problem for the Freudian reading of the story is that, while the children do not see the ghosts, the reader does. James invoked the evil and haunting presence of the dead Peter Quint and Miss Jessel with consummate zeal and energy. He managed to have it both ways. The ghosts existed, it is true, only in the mind of the governess; the ghosts, more importantly, also give the reader the creeps.

For anyone thinking of making a film of the story, this ambiguity was a godsend. All you needed was a suggestive, vulnerable, and sexually repressed lead actress ("I played it as if she were completely sane," Kerr said [Loban and Valley]), a lot of wild music, and some special effects as the ghosts peered in windows or stood on the battlements of the remote house.

The black and white film, directed by Jack Clayton, is quite beautiful. It too is framed at the beginning, in this case by the appearance of Deborah Kerr's pleading hands and face, wonderfully lit. She is filmed from the side and insists rather too emphatically for comfort that she loves the children and only wants to care for them. The spooky atmosphere of the house is re-created with great subtlety (no cheap shock tactics or easy effects). Megs Jenkins plays the deeply stupid housekeeper Mrs. Grose as conscientious and kind-hearted and knowing her place. Slowly, as the camera moves from wide scenes of faded opulence to tiny and frightening objects, Mrs. Grose's expression becomes permanently worried and bewildered; she unwillingly reveals that the two dead servants, Peter Quint and Miss Jessel, were less than innocent.

While in the Broadway play of the story the children actually see the ghosts and in Britten's opera Miles and Flora sing to them, here their innocence is ambiguously preserved. They do not see what appears so dreadful and appalling to their overwrought governess. But they are not all sweetness and light either. The sense that they have been cor-rupted, or that there is an extraordinary bond between them, is carefully dramatized.

In James's story, there is no explanation given for Miles's expulsion from school. In the 1974 television version, he is naughty and knowing and tor-tures animals; he is a fourteen-year-old boy who flirts with his governess, kissing her in one bedroom scene. In the story, when the governess comes to his bedroom, Miles blows her candle out. (This is repeated in Britten's opera: "T'was I who blew it, who blew it, dear!" [Britten 246].) And in *The Innocents*, even though Miles, played by Martin Stephens, looks like a nine-year-old, he is not beyond coming on to his governess, his kisses seeming deliberate and sexual rather than innocent and sweet.

This causes the governess to believe even more that the children have been corrupted as she makes mad plans to send Flora to her uncle, played with an amused camp glint in his eye by Michael Redgrave. She wants to stay with Miles to confront the ghastly Quint. As she becomes more and more hysterical, it is clear why Pauline Kael called *The Innocents* "the best ghost movie I've ever seen" (McClelland 20) and easy to mourn the fact that Henry James, when he finally took up residence at Lamb House, did not have a DVD player in his drawing room, all the more to frighten him so that he would, once more, be afraid to go to bed.

WORKS BY HENRY JAMES

BB   *Beloved Boy: Letters to Hendrik C. Anderson, 1899–1915*. Ed. Rosella Mamoli Zorzi. Charlottesville: U of Virginia P, 2004.

CN   *The Complete Notebooks of Henry James*. Ed. Leon Edel and Lyall H. Powers. New York: Oxford UP, 1987.

HJL   *Henry James Letters*. Ed. Leon Edel. Vol. 4. Cambridge: Belknap P of Harvard UP, 1984.

LHJ   *The Letters of Henry James*. Ed. Percy Lubbock. New York: Scribner, 1920.

TS   *The Turn of the Screw*. Ed. Deborah Esch and Jonathan Warren. 2nd. ed. New York: Norton, 1999.

OTHER WORKS CITED

Britten, Benjamin. *The Turn of the Screw, Op. 54, An Opera in a Prologue and Two Acts. Libretto, after the story by Henry James, by Myfanwy Piper*. London: Hawkes, 1966.

Gosse, Edmund. *Aspects and Impressions*. London: Cassell, 1922.

Loban, Leila, and Richard Valley. "Interview with Deborah Kerr." *Scarlet Street* 21 (1995): 51–52.

McClelland, Doug. *The Unkindest Cuts: The Scissors and the Cinema*. New York: Barnes, 1972.

Phelps, William Lyon. *The Advance of the English Novel*. New York: Dodd, 1916.

FILMOGRAPHY

The Innocents (U.S.). Screenplay by William Archibald and Truman Capote, additional dialogue provided by John Mortimer. Dir. Jack Clayton. Photog. Freddie Francis. Music by Georges Auric. Ed. James Clark. Perf. Deborah Kerr (Miss Giddens/Governess), Michael Redgrave (Uncle), Megs Jenkins (Mrs. Grose), Martin Stephens (Miles), Pamela Franklin (Flora), Peter Wyngarde (Peter Quint), Clytie Jessop (Miss Mary Jessel), Eric Woodburn (Coachman), Isla Cameron (Anna). CinemaScope–Twentieth-Century Fox/Achilles, bw, 99 mins., 1961.

The Nightcomers (U.S.). A "prequel" to James's "The Turn of the Screw," focusing on Quint and Jessel's relationship. Screenplay by Michael Hastings. Dir. Michael Winner. Photog. Robert Paynter. Music by Jerry Fielding. Perf. Marlon Brando (Peter Quint), Stephanie Beachum (Miss Margaret Jessel), Thora Hird (Mrs. Grose), Verna Harvey (Flora), Christopher Ellis (Miles), Harry Andrews (Master of the House), Anna Palk (New Governess). Scimitar/AE, Technicolor, 96 mins., 1971. LC.

The Others. Screenplay by Alejandro Amenábar. Dir. Alejandro Amenábar. Perf. Nicole Kidman (Grace Stewart), Finnula Flanagan (Mrs. Bertha Mills), Christopher Ecceleston (Charles Stewart), Alakina Mann (Anne Stewart), James Bentley (Nicholas Stewart), Eric Sykes (Mr. Edmund Tuttle), Elaine Cassidy (Lydia). Cruise/Wagner Productions, 101 mins., 2001.

The Turn of the Screw (U.S.; TV). Teleplay by William F. Nolan. Dir. Dan Curtis. Photog. Colin Callow. Music by Robert Cobert. Ed. Bill Breashers, Gary Anderson. Perf. Lynn Redgrave (Jane Cubberly/Governess), Jasper Jacob (Miles), James Laurenson (Peter Quint), Eva Griffith (Flora), Megs

Jenkins (Mrs. Grose), Kathryn Leigh Schott (Miss Jessel), Benedict Taylor (Timothy), John Baron (Fredericks), Vivian Bennet (Secretary). Dan Curtis Productions, two-part series, color, 118 mins., 1974. Videocassette. MPI Home Video, 1992. LC.

CHAPTER FIVE

The Lessons of the Master

Philip Larkin, in his poem "Dockery and Son," which was written in 1963 when Larkin was forty-one, wrote about a situation that would also preoccupy Henry James in his forties, the situation of being single and childless. In "Dockery and Son," the poet discovers that Dockery, "that withdrawn / High-collared public schoolboy" who was junior to him at college, must have had a son when aged nineteen or twenty. As the poet travels away, he thinks about his own fate: "To have no son, no wife, / No house or land still seemed quite natural" (lines 16–17, 25–26). Dockery clearly thought that "adding meant increase" whereas to the poet "it was dilution" (lines 34, 35).

On January 5, 1888, when Henry James was in his mid-forties, he recorded a conversation with the journalist Theodore Child in his notebook "about the effect of marriage on the artist, the man of letters, etc. He mentioned the cases he had seen in Paris in which this effect had been fatal to the quality of the work, etc.—through overproduction, need to meet expenses, make a figure, etc. And I mentioned certain cases here" (CN 43).

Child spoke of the French novelist Alphonse Daudet, whom James also knew, saying of his 30 Ans de Paris, a memoir, that "he would never have written that if he hadn't married" (qtd. in CN 43). James then wrote:

> So it occurred to me that a very interesting situation would be that of an elder artist or writer, who had been ruined (in his own sight) by his marriage and its forcing him to produce promiscuously and cheaply— his position in regard to a younger confrère whom he sees on the brink of the same disaster and whom he endeavours to save, to rescue, by some act of bold interference—breaking off the marriage, annihilating the wife, making trouble between the parties. (43–44)

As a result of this conversation, James was inspired to write his story "The Lesson of the Master," published later that year.

Four years earlier, James had had a similar conversation with Edmund Gosse about John Addington Symonds, "of his extreme and somewhat hysterical aestheticism" and of his wife's disapproving of the tone of her husband's work, "thinking his books immoral, pagan, hyper-aesthetic, etc." (*CN* 25). He imagined Symonds's wife saying: "I have never read any of John's works. I think them most *undesirable*." James immediately saw a drama he could make between "the narrow, cold, Calvinistic wife, a rigid moralist; and the husband, impregnated—even to morbidness—with the spirit of Italy, the love of beauty, of art." From these seeds he grew "The Author of Beltraffio," the first of the ten stories he wrote about writers.

In both cases James brought in two other characters besides the writer and his wife; in both stories there was a younger man, an admirer of the older writer's work, and in both also an innocent younger person over whose future there will be a battle. In the case of "The Author of Beltraffio," this person was the young son of the writer and his Puritan wife; in "The Lesson of the Master" it was a young woman, Marian Fancourt.

All of his life as a writer James worried about both the purity of his work and the making of money. It was as though he himself were a married couple. One part of him cared for the fullness of art and the other part for the fullness of the cupboard. James sought both with stubborn steadfast zeal. Sometimes when he realized that he could not achieve one without failing the other, he argued with himself. However, he seldom gave up trying to wed them. James struck hard bargains with publishers and editors. His notebooks are full of hopeful jottings of ideas that might not only come to full fruition as works of art but as objects that would take the measure, as he called it, of the great flat foot of the public.

The argument between moral and artistic principles and between commerce and art interested James deeply, and it might have been enough for him to intensify this argument in pure drama, make it as simple as the row between a husband and a wife over the publication of a book, or the direction of a career. In both "The Author of Beltraffio" and "The Lesson of the Master," it seems at first that this will be his subject, as observed by the younger man, the admirer. But in "The Lesson of the Master" James sought not only to allow his master-writer Henry St. George to teach two different lessons to the younger man—one about art, and the other about everything—but he sought also to show the reader his own mastery of the ambiguous line, the ironic drama surrounding complex motive and plot twist. He wished to make clear that the Master was not only Henry St. George but Henry James.

James thought highly enough of "The Lesson of the Master" to include it in the New York Edition of his work, published in 1909, from which he excluded the majority of his tales and stories. In his introduction to the volume in which "Lesson" is included, James set out to justify his use of a character who was eminent, such as the famous writer Henry St. George. "I'm not ashamed to allow," he wrote, "it was *amusing* to make these people 'great,' so far as one could do so without making them intrinsically false" (*FW* 1231). To the reader who wished to know on whom he had based Henry St. George, James insisted that he could not tell. "[A]nd it would n't indeed do for me to name his exemplar publicly even were I able. But I none the less maintain his situation to have been in *essence* an observed reality" (1230–31).

The truth was, of course, that the story arose from what James heard about Daudet—as always, he loved hearing half a story so that his imagination could work on the rest. He filled in the detail and worked on the form using what he knew best, which was himself. As Fred Kaplan has pointed out in *Henry James: The Imagination of Genius*, James was never to earn as much money as he did in 1888, the year of "The Lesson of the Master," publishing and producing an enormous and uneven quantity of work. His name was everywhere, but he remained both the Henry St. George of earlier days, "a high literary figure" as Paul Overt sees him, and the figure by whom Overt is disappointed because of "the lower range of production to which he had fallen after his three first great successes, the comparative absence of quality in his later work" (*CS* 545).

Thus James allowed St. George to appear as a metaphor for his own presence in the literary world, just as Overt, by renouncing what he most desired and working with high ambition, believing love to be a dilution of his talent, also represented James in one of his guises. Both men dreamed of love, and it was these dreams that James guarded carefully in London in the 1880s. He gave to his characters all the more intensely what he renounced himself. A decade later these dreams and desires would emerge in his letters to younger men such as Hendrik Andersen and Jocelyn Persse. But for the moment, the Master's imagination allowed his readers to know that the lesson for anyone seeking fame as a writer could be learned in the indeterminate space between the bossy Mrs. St. George and the lovely Marian Fancourt, or in the solitary cage of renouncing love for the sake of art and living with the consequences.

WORKS BY HENRY JAMES

CN   *The Complete Notebooks of Henry James.* Ed. Leon Edel and Lyall H. Powers. New York: Oxford UP, 1987.

CS   *Complete Stories 1884–1891.* New York: Library of America, 1999.

FW   *French Writers, Other European Writers, the Prefaces to the New York Edition.* Ed. Leon Edel. New York: Library of America, 1984. Vol. 2 of *Literary Criticism.*

CHAPTER SIX

Henry James's New York

Most of James's contemporaries wrote about him, leaving accounts of his extraordinary mannerisms and ticks of speech. One of the most interesting was by John Buchan, Lord Tweedsmuir, the author of *The Thirty-Nine Steps*, in his autobiography *Memory Hold-the-Door*. His first memory of James belongs to the general folklore surrounding the novelist. James was at dinner in a country house and was informed that the Madeira was very special. "He sipped his glass," Buchan wrote, "and his large benign face remained impassive while he gave his verdict. I wish I could remember his epithets; they were a masterpiece of the intricate, evasive and noncommittal, and yet of an exquisite politeness" (151). The Madeira, it turned out, had been sold by a dishonest butler and replaced by cheap stuff from a neighboring public house. James had, it seemed, made his position clear without saying anything to insult his hosts. The outline of Buchan's anecdote is repeated over and over in the memoirs of the time.

Buchan's second anecdote, however, is more telling and offers one of the best and most original insights into James. An aunt of Buchan's wife, the widow of Byron's grandson, asked James and Buchan to examine her archives "in order to reach some conclusion on the merits of the quarrel between Byron and his wife. She thought," Buchan wrote, "that those particular papers might be destroyed by some successor and she wanted a statement of their contents deposited in the British Museum." So the two eminent Victorians "waded," in Buchan's words, "through masses of ancient indecency." The thing, he wrote, "nearly made me sick, but my colleague never turned a hair." As they came across the more indecent passages, Buchan wrote, James's only words for some special vileness were "singular" and "most curious" and "nauseating, perhaps, but how quite inexpressibly significant" (151–52).

James, when he contemplated human behavior, was not a typical Vic-

torian prude. He found treachery and greed and straying from the narrow too interesting, too intrinsically dramatic, to be debased by mere
judgment. But everything in James is ambiguous and complex, so it is
important to emphasize that while he did not judge humans harshly or go
in for crude forms of disapproval, he did not stretch that lenient attitude
to art. He judged books and paintings and architecture as harshly as he
pleased, and at times even more harshly, just as he made sure to praise the
books and pictures and buildings that he loved. He was tolerant of bad
humans, intolerant of bad art.

Music did not interest him much, but painting did a great deal. He
took a benign, if rather offensively patronizing, view of the American
need for European paintings. In 1874 he wrote:

> It has been proved that there is no reason in the essence of things why a
> room full of old masters should not be walked into from an American
> street and appear to proper advantage in spite of what in harmonious
> phrase we suppose we should call its location. There is something we
> like, moreover, in our sending out at a venture for half a million dollars'
> worth of pictorial entertainment. (*PE* 87)

Paintings play a large part in James's fiction, just as looking at paintings
and writing about them occupied his time, especially when he was young.
He reserved some of his greatest disapproving moments for paintings he
did not like. These included a painting by the French painter Gérôme of
a cock fight, which James saw in Boston when he was twenty-nine. "A
young man," James wrote,

> entirely naked, is stooping upon one knee, and stirring two bristling
> game-cocks to battle. A young woman, also naked—more than naked,
> as one somehow feels Gérôme's figures to be—reclines beside him
> and looks lazily on. . . . There is a total lack of what we may call moral
> atmosphere. . . . The horrid little game in the centre, the brassy nudity
> of the youth, the peculiarly sensible carnality of the young woman, the
> happy combination of moral and physical shamelessness, spiced with
> the most triumphant cleverness, conduce to an impression from which
> no element of interest is absent, save the good old-fashioned sense of
> being pleased. (*PE* 51)

So, too, in a long 1872 essay on the collection that became the germ of the Metropolitan Museum of Art, a collection which James believed "contains no first-rate example of a first-rate genius" (52), James stood in front of a painting by Jacob Jordaens and commented: "The Virgin is a sweet-faced young woman whom the painter evidently meant to make pretty within the limits of Flemish probability, and the child has an odd look of having just waked up the least bit cross from a nap" (54). Two years later, from Florence, he had this to say about Rubens:

> Was Rubens lawfully married to Nature, or did he merely keep up the most unregulated of flirtations? Three or four of his great carnal cataracts ornament the walls of the Pitti. If the union was really solemnized it must be said that the ménage was at best a stormy one. He is a strangely irresponsible jumble of the true and the false. He paints a full flesh surface that radiates and palpitates with illusion, and into the midst of it he thrusts a mouth, a nose, an eye, which you would call your latest-born a blockhead for perpetrating. (20)

But, as time went on, the enemy ceased to be the limits of Flemish probability and became the limits of painting itself as James began to see Impressionism as his enemy. In 1876 James saw an early showing of the work of Renoir, Monet, Sisley, Pisarro, and Morisot. "[T]his little band," he wrote in a dispatch to the *New York Tribune*,

> is on all grounds less interesting than the group out of which Millais and Holman Hunt rose into fame. None of its members show signs of possessing first-rate talent, and indeed the "Impressionist" doctrines strike me as incompatible, in an artist's mind, with the existence of first-rate talent. . . . [T]he Impressionists . . . abjure virtue altogether, and declare that a subject which has been crudely chosen shall be loosely treated. They send detail to the dogs and concentrate themselves on general expression. (*PE* 114–15)

In his writing about painting Henry James made many statements. "There is no greater work of art than a great portrait" (227). Or "a picture should have some relation to life as well as to painting" (143). Or "a picture is not an impression but an expression—just as a poem or a piece of music is" (165). There is a sense of his eyes as engaged and exacting, just as there is a sense of deep disapproval of any European pictures making their way in groups to the United States. As he lived in Europe, James came to see civilization as a slow, gradual process, which could not, despite the efforts of his fellow countrymen, be bought and then shipped home. He came to believe that civilization would come too late to his native country for him to witness, or that it would be barbarous when it came. His views on painting, as most of his views on society and politics, tended to oppose change and cherish what was stable and unalarming. His interest in stability bordered at times on the strange, the neurotic.

Very early in his career as a writer he made his position clear. He would not be a public novelist nor a social commentator but would instead deal with the reverse of the picture. The intricacies and vagaries of feeling in the relations between people, and mainly between men and women, would be his subject. Duplicity and greed, disappointment and renunciation, which became his most pressing themes, occurred for James the novelist in the private realm. It was his genius to make this realm seem more dramatic and ample than any space inhabited by government or business.

James himself was a figure of complexity and ambiguity and secrecy; a number of matters in his life seem greatly unresolved. His personality, like his later prose style, was one in which things could not be easily named, in which nuance was more substantial than fact and the flickering of consciousness more interesting than knowledge. James was, above all, guarded. He was the supreme artist concerned with the architecture and tone of fiction; he specialized in the deliberate, the considered, and the exertion of control; he did not seek to bare his soul for the reader.

Nonetheless, it is possible to read between the lines of James's work, searching for clues, seeking moments in which the author came close to unmasking himself. Many of his stories, written quickly and for money, give more away perhaps than he intended. Here, more than in the novels, he comes closer to opening a chink, for example, in the grand armor of his own sexuality, allowing us to catch a brief glimpse of his deepest and darkest concerns. These stories include "The Pupil," "The Author of Beltraffio," and "The Beast in the Jungle." The stories are careful and restrained but make clear that the subject of illicit love or misguided loyalty interested James deeply, as did the subject of sexual coldness.

We can trace James's sometimes unwitting, unconscious, and often quite deliberate efforts to mask and explore matters that concerned him deeply and uneasily. We could trace, for example, in his copious writings, all references to Ireland or England, or to his brother William, or to the novelist George Eliot and find areas of ambiguity and uncertainty as well as strange contradictions, underlining the fact that these things mattered very profoundly to James, so profoundly indeed that they appear in many layers and guises.

Perhaps of all the provinces in his realm whose contours remain shadowy and whose topography is unresolved, the city of New York is the prime example. James's writings about New York disclose, more than anything, an anger, quite unlike any other anger in James, at what has been lost to him, what has been done, in the name of commerce and material progress, to a place he once knew. His is not an ordinary anger at the destruction of beauty and familiarity; it is much stranger than that, and it deserves a great deal of attention.

There is a peculiar intensity in the tone of Henry James's memoir of his first fourteen years, *A Small Boy and Others*, written in 1911, when James was sixty-eight, one year after the death of his brother William. Much of the memory evoked and most of the scenes conjured up in the book took place in New York between 1848, when the Jameses moved to the city, and 1855, when they left for Europe. Since he had no notes or letters or diaries to work from, it is astonishing how fresh and detailed his memory is, how many names he can remember, including those of teachers and actors, how sharply he can evoke places and their atmospheres, precise smells and sights and locations, including many shows and plays in the New York theaters of the time. "I have lost nothing of what I saw," he wrote, "and that though I can't now quite divide the total into separate occasions the various items surprisingly swarm for me" (*AU* 60).

It was as though Old New York, as he saw it between the ages of five and twelve, had remained still and frozen and perfect in his memory. He had not watched it change, nor participated in its growth. New York was the ground that formed him; he was never to have a place again that would belong to him so fundamentally. He would not possess another territory until 1897, when he signed the lease on Lamb House in Rye in England. The fact that his New York had been taken from him and not replaced, save by hotel rooms and temporary abodes, may explain the sheer driven enthusiasm with which he pursued Lamb House and his sense of relief when he had made it his. Indeed, the year before James purchased the lease he wrote his novel *The Spoils of Poynton*, a drama about owning and losing a treasured house. Having signed the lease, he wrote "The Turn of the Screw" about a lone figure attempting to make a home in a house already possessed.

New York after 1855 was lost to James, not merely, he realized as the years went on, by his father's removing the family to Europe, but by changes in the city that would be absolute and overwhelming. A new world was being built on the site of his dreams. Its most hallowed quarter was Number 58 West Fourteenth Street, first seen during "an afternoon call with my father at a house there situated, one of an already fairly mature row on the south side and quite near Sixth Avenue. It was 'our' house, just acquired by us. . . . the place was to become to me for ever so long afterwards a sort of anchorage of the spirit" (*AU* 57).

Henry James's New York, the city of his childhood, "the small warm dusky homogeneous New York world of the mid-century," was situated between Fifth and Sixth Avenues down to Washington Square, where his maternal grandmother lived, and up eastwards to Union Square, which was, in his day, surrounded by a high railing (38). Close by were members of James's extended family, including his mother's cousin Helen. "I see in her strong simplicity," he wrote, "that of an earlier, quieter world, a New York of better manners and better morals and homelier beliefs" (71). James saw that "her goodness somehow testifies for the whole tone of a society, a remarkable cluster of private decencies." His book became an elegy not only to a lost childhood, but a set of values which began to erode as soon as the village James could wander in freely was replaced by a great city. "[C]haracter," he wrote about these changes, "is so lost in quantity" (117–18).

As James grew older he was allowed to wander farther. He remembered

hard by the Fourteenth Street home . . . the poplars, the pigs, the poultry, and the "Irish houses," two or three in number, exclusive of a very fine Dutch one, seated then, this last, almost as among gardens and

groves—a breadth of territory still apparent, on the spot, in that mar-
ginal ease, that spread of occupation, to the nearly complete absence of
which New York aspects owe their general failure of "style." (58)

He and his brother wandered up and down Broadway "like perfect little
men of the world; we must have been let loose there to stretch our legs
and fill our lungs, without prejudice either to our earlier and later free-
doms of going and coming. . . . Broadway must have been then as one of
the alleys of Eden" (116).

In this city, a mixture of a remembered Eden and a failed style, James
set more than half a dozen stories and one novel; he also devoted considerable space to New York in *The American Scene*, written several years
before his autobiography. In his fiction, James did not set out to chart the
history of the city or the emotion surrounding its growth. What he disclosed about his attitude toward New York he did in passing. In the foreground were his characters, more real and more pressing in their needs
than mere bricks and mortar.

As his own scope as a writer widened and his ambition hardened,
Henry James became, at times, acutely alert to the thinness of the American experience. In his book on Hawthorne, written in 1879, he famously
listed what was absent in American life:

> No sovereign, no court, no personal loyalty, no aristocracy, no church,
> no clergy, no army, no diplomatic service, no country gentlemen, no
> palaces, no castles, nor manors, nor old country-houses, nor parson-
> ages, nor thatched cottages nor ivied ruins; no cathedrals, nor abbeys,
> nor little Norman churches; no great Universities nor public schools—
> no Oxford, nor Eton, nor Harrow; no literature, no novels, no muse-
> ums, no pictures, no political society, no sporting class. . . . (*EL* 351)

Seven years earlier, however, in a letter to Charles Eliot Norton, he had
written: "It's a complex fate, being an American, and one of the responsibilities it entails is fighting against a superstitious valuation of Europe"
(*HJL* 1: 274).

James worked then in the interstices between America as a wasteland,
untouched by tradition, and America as a golden opportunity for a novelist interested in complexity. In his first New York story, "The Story of

a Masterpiece," published in the magazine *Galaxy* in 1868, when James was twenty-five, his hero can be a man of taste and the city a place where such a man will rub shoulders with artists, one of whom will paint "the best portrait that has yet been painted in America" (*CS1* 235). James will also begin to display in some of his fiction a view of women as somehow untrustworthy and of love as a loss of balance. In this story, the painter manages to catch the true nature of Marian Everett, which causes John Lennox, her suitor, to destroy the painting. "The Story of a Masterpiece" was welcomed by *The Nation*: "within the narrow limits to which he confines himself Mr James is the best writer of short stories in America" (*CT* 20).

By this time James had only written six of those short stories. The two most substantial of these, "The Story of a Year" and "Poor Richard," concerned the aftermath of the Civil War, more precisely the relationship between the men who had fought in the war and the women who stayed at home. James's ninth story, "A Most Extraordinary Case," published in the *Atlantic Monthly* in April 1868, dramatized that same subject.

The story opens in New York, in "one of the uppermost chambers" of one of its "great" hotels (*CS1* 263). Mason, whose injuries in the war, while grave, remain unspecified, is living in an "ugly little hotel chamber." This is one of James's New York stories where it is imperative for the protagonist to leave the city, which is too lonely or unhealthy or just too hot. James cannot imagine anyone recovering from anything in the city he had lost, therefore he moves Mason to a house on the Hudson River. Miss Hoffman, his hostess's niece, "looks as if she had come out of an American novel. I don't know that that's great praise," to which Mason replies: "You're bound in honor, then . . . to put her into another" (271). The heroine in question is notable because she inspired James's most un-American sentence in his career thus far: "She was now twenty-six years of age, beautiful, accomplished, and *au mieux* with her bankers" (273).

James, as he developed as a novelist, became seriously *au mieux* with the recognition scene, in which a character watches an encounter between two people from a distance and, by their gestures and movements and silences, realizes what is between them. This scenario offers us the central drama of both *The Portrait of a Lady* and *The Ambassadors*. In "A Most Extraordinary Case," written when he was twenty-five, James tries the scene out for the first time. Entering a room, Mason, now recovering with the help of a talented young doctor, notices Miss Hoffman at the piano while "[a] gentleman was leaning on the instrument with his back toward the window, intercepting her face. . . . The silence was unnatural, or, at the least, disagreeable" (278). This gentleman is the doctor who will eventually win Miss Hoffman's hand. Toward the end of the story, Mason will catch "a glance of intelligence" between the two, and the knowledge of the deep bond between them will hasten his decline (291).

In this story, as in "The Story of a Year," the business of injury and illness interests James. Illness will surface in a great deal of his work, in the case of Ralph Touchett in *The Portrait of a Lady* and Milly Theale in *The Wings of a Dove*. Although Mason's wounds were caused by the Civil War, and resemble those of Oliver Wendell Holmes, his recovery depends on his happiness, and his decline will be caused by unrequited love. In James's early world it was still possible to die of a broken heart. "A Most Extraordinary Case" won the approval of James's harshest critic throughout his career, his brother William. "[Y]our style grows easier, firmer," he wrote, "and more concise as you go on writing . . . the face of the whole story is bright and sparkling" (Edel, *Untried* 246).

"Crawford's Consistency," James's next New York story, was published in *Scribner's Monthly* in August 1876, a few months before he moved from Paris to London. For that and "The Ghostly Rental" he was paid three hundred dollars. "I have lately sent two short tales to Scribner," he wrote to his father in April 1876 from his address at the Rue du Luxembourg, "which you will see when they are printed, and I trust judge according to their pretensions, which are very small" (*HJL* 2: 39). James did not include "Crawford's Consistency" in any single volume in his lifetime. Here, as in his memoir, he plays the elegiac note, setting the story in the 1840s. When Crawford and the narrator take a walk into the countryside, the narrator remarks, for example, "for in those days New Yorkers could walk out into the country" (*CS2* 154).

In those days Crawford was a man with a fortune about to marry the beautiful but penniless Miss Ingram, who had always inspired the narrator "with a vague mistrust" (126). Miss Ingram finally jilts Crawford and then comes down with smallpox whereupon James allows his narrator one of his most unpleasant observations. "Several months afterward," he wrote, "I saw the young girl, shrouded in a thick veil, beneath which I could just distinguish her absolutely blasted face. On either side of her walked her father and mother, each of them showing a visage almost as blighted as her own" (155).

Crawford marries unsuitably, and, having lost his fortune, becomes prey to his wife, who pushes him down a set of steps, breaking his leg. The narrator believes that he can never go back to her, but, like Isabel Archer in *The Portrait of a Lady*, which James began a few years after the composition of "Crawford's Consistency," the protagonist returns to the spouse, renouncing the possibility of easy freedom.

"An International Episode," a sort of companion piece to "Daisy Miller," which had appeared six months earlier, was first published in *Cornhill Magazine* in December 1878 and January 1879. Two young Englishmen, one the heir to a title and a fortune, come to New York and experience the city in the stifling heat of summer. They are great blank creations, almost stupid at times, alert only to their own station and the newness and strangeness of the New World. The hot summer allows James to follow the routine he had already developed in "A Most Extraordinary Case" and make the city a site to begin the story but not a place where a narrative could unfold. The Englishmen's contact in New York, J. L. Westgate, is one of James's few creations who actually has a job, who puts in a full day at the office. Westgate's wife and sister-in-law are at Newport, and the reader can feel James itching to remove his two young men from the "sinister hum of mosquitoes" (*CS2* 329) in the inhospitable city to Newport, away from the world of J. L. Westgate and his money-making activities to the world of leisure and American women, led by Westgate's sister-in-law Miss Alden. These women are forward, intelligent, charming, curious, and opinionated, ripe for a young English lord, who is used to more stuffy company, to fall in love with.

Miss Alden is Daisy Miller's opposite. She is too intelligent to be doomed. If she breaks the rules, it is due to her genuine lack of respect for them rather than any weakness. The English are seen in the story as snobbish, thoughtless, bad mannered, a race on whom everything is lost. The Americans are democratic and hospitable. When the story appeared, it was roundly attacked by Mrs. F. H. Hill, the wife of the editor of the *Daily News*, who James knew socially in London. "Mrs. Hill," Leon Edel writes, "accused James of caricaturing the British nobility, and of putting language into its mouth which it would never utter. Henry on this occasion replied, since he knew the lady, and the letter is a magisterial defense of his work and his art. It is the only letter extant which he wrote to a reviewer" (Edel, *Conquest* 316).

"A man in my position," James wrote to Mrs. Hill,

and writing the sort of things I do, feels the need of protesting against this extension of his idea in which in many cases, many readers are certain to indulge. One may make figures and figures without intending generalizations—generalizations of which I have a horror. I make a couple of English ladies do a disagreeable thing—*cela c'est vu*: excuse me!—and forthwith I find myself responsible for a representation of English manners! Nothing is my *last word* about anything—I am interminably supersubtle and analytic—and with the blessing of heaven, I shall live to make all sorts of representations of all sorts of things. It will take a much cleverer person than myself to discover my last impression—among all these things—of anything. And then, in such a matter, the bother of being an American! Trollope, Thackaray, Dickens, even with their big authoritative talents, were free to draw all sorts of unflattering English pictures, by the thousand. But if I make a single one, I am forthwith in danger of being confronted with a criminal conclusion—and sinister rumours reach me as to what I think of English society. I think more things than I can undertake to tell in forty pages of the *Cornhill*. Perhaps some day I shall take more pages, and attempt to tell some of these things; in that case, I hope, there will be a little, of every sort, for every one! Meanwhile I shall draw plenty of pictures of disagreeable Americans, as I have done already, and the friendly Briton will see no harm in that!—it will seem to him a part of the natural fitness! (*HJL* 2: 221–22)

On 4 January 1879, James wrote about the matter to Grace Norton in Boston: "You may be interested to know that I hear my little 'International Episode' has given offence to various people of my acquaintance here. Don't you wonder at it? So long as one serves up Americans for their entertainment it is all right—but hands off the sacred natives! They are really I think, thinner-skinned than we!" (*HJL* 2: 209). Two weeks later,

James wrote to his mother: "It seems to me myself that I have been very delicate; but I shall keep off dangerous ground in future" (213).

Later that year, when he published his book on Hawthorne, James discovered that Americans could also be thin skinned. He was attacked by critics in both New York and Boston ("the clucking of a brood of prairie-hens," he called them [*HJL* 2: 280]), including his friend William Dean Howells, whose tone was milder but whose opinion was pointed: "We foresee, without any powerful prophetic lens, that Mr. James will be in some quarters promptly attainted of high treason" (Edel, *Conquest* 389). To the accusation that Hawthorne was provincial, Howells responded: "If it is not provincial for an Englishman to be English, or a Frenchman French, then it is not so for an American to be American; and if Hawthorne was 'exquisitely provincial' one had better take one's chance of universality with him than with almost any Londoner or Parisian of his time." He sent James his review.

James was unrepentant. He replied:

> I think it is extremely provincial for a Russian to be very Russian, a Portuguese very Portuguese; for the simple reason that certain national types are essentially and intrinsically provincial. I sympathize even less with your protest against the idea that it takes an old civilization to set a novelist in motion—a proposition that seems to me so true as to be a truism. (*HJL* 2: 267)

In that same letter James mentioned a forthcoming serialization in the *Cornhill* magazine of "a poorish story in three numbers—a tale purely American, the writing of which made me feel acutely the want of the 'paraphernalia'" (268).

The paraphernalia in question were, James had written earlier in the letter, the "manners, customs, usages, habits, forms, upon all these things matured and established, that a novelist lives—they are the very stuff his work is made of" (267). The "poorish story" was *Washington Square*. While James was being modest when he mentioned the book to Howells (and his general tendency in referring to his own work was to be self-deprecating), it still must seem that he underestimated the book. *Washington Square* is certainly his best short novel and remains among his best books. The first of his books to be serialized simultaneously on both sides of the

Atlantic, it offered him the freedom to devote a great deal of time to *The Portrait of a Lady*, his next project.

Washington Square tells the story of Dr. Sloper and his only daughter Catherine, whom he considers dull. When Catherine falls in love with a penniless young man, her father becomes determined, in ways that are cold and cruel, that his daughter must not marry the interloper. James's portrait of the vulnerable, sensitive, and unassertive daughter is one of the most sustained and convincing of his career. The value of *Washington Square* also lies in how the lack of "paraphernalia" forces James to intensify the psychology, to draw the father and daughter with greater subtlety and care. At the apex of his social power in London, James did not know enough about the city and the society in which he had set the novel. He knew about the interior of the houses where he had been a small boy; he could write about familiar rooms; but he had not grown up in that world enough to know its wider personality.

James placed the events of *Washington Square* in the very years when he and his family were living in the city; he made his grandmother's house become Dr. Sloper's house, as a year later he would make his other grandmother's house become Isabel Archer's house in Albany. The original story was told to him by Fanny Kemble, whose brother had jilted an heiress when he discovered that her father intended to disinherit her. James moved this story to his own lost territory, to the site which belonged now merely to his dreams, to Old New York, whose contours he had barely made out before he was removed from it. In chapter 2 of the book he inserted a passage about Washington Square and its environs that strikes the reader as strange, almost clumsy, and unthinkable for a novelist who is about to write *The Portrait of a Lady*.

"I know not," he wrote of the area around the square,

> whether it is owing to the tenderness of early associations, but this portion of New York appears to many persons the most delectable. It has a kind of established repose which is not of frequent occurrence in other quarters of the long, shrill city; it has a riper, richer, more honourable look than any of the upper ramifications of the great longitudinal thoroughfare—the look of having had something of a social history. . . . it was here that your grandmother lived, in venerable solitude,

and dispensed a hospitality which commended itself alike to the infant imagination and the infant palate; it was here that you took your first walks abroad, following the nursery-maid with unequal step. . . . It was here, finally, that your first school, kept by a broad-bosomed, broad-based old lady with a ferule, who was always having tea in a blue cup, with a saucer that didn't match, enlarged the circle both of your observations and your sensations. It was here, at any rate, that my heroine spent many years of her life; which is my excuse for this topographical parenthesis. (*NO* 15–16)

This may well be the excuse, but it is hardly the reason. The reason is that, a quarter of a century after it had been lost to him, James was prepared to disrupt the sacred seamlessness of his fiction to evoke this square as belonging to his own memory, his primary sense of self that could be brought back now only in words. The need was so pressing and urgent that he would allow such a paragraph to remain; had it been about another place, he would surely have removed it. He was claiming Washington Square for himself. It was here also, soon afterwards, that he began to evoke the next generation, who were too ready to eschew social history for the blight, as James saw it, of newness.

Dr. Sloper's niece, for example, is about to marry Arthur Townsend, who speaks about his new house:

it's only for three or four years. At the end of three or four years we'll move. That's the way to live in New York—to move every three or four years. Then you always get the last thing. It's because the city's growing so quick—you've got to keep up with it. It's going straight up town— that's where New York's going. . . . I guess we'll move up little by little; when we get tired of one street we'll go higher. So you see we'll always have a new house; it's a great advantage to have a new house; you get all the latest improvements. They invent everything all over again about every five years, and it's a great thing to keep up with the new things. (26)

It is easy to feel James's rage and exasperation at the new ethos of quick change that has eaten up his city of old values, destroyed the few buildings and streets with many rich old associations for him. Like the passage quoted above about Washington Square itself, however, this long speech by the young man seems forced and makes its point rather too heavily. These two passages stand out in a novel that is otherwise compact and tightly constructed. They are part of James's deeply irrational response to the New York he had known and to what had replaced it; his emotions about the city, as about no other place, moved at times slowly and strangely out of his control.

Three years later, after the death of his parents and a return to the United States, James wrote another story set in New York, "The Impressions of a Cousin," one of his slackest and weakest stories but interesting nonetheless for the further light it shines on his attitude to New York. The story opens as the narrator wonders how she can inhabit Fifty-third Street. "When I turn into it from Fifth Avenue the vista seems too hideous; the narrow, impersonal houses, with the dry, hard tone of their brown-stone, a surface as uninteresting as that of sandpaper; their steep, stiff stoops, giving you such a climb to the door; their lumpish balustrades, porticoes, and cornices, turned out by the hundred and adorned with heavy excrescences—such an eruption of ornament and such a poverty of effect!" (*CS2* 650). The narrator is a painter, returned from Italy, who remarks in the early pages that there is nothing to sketch in the city, not even the people. "What people? the people in the Fifth Avenue? They are even less pictorial than their houses. I don't perceive that those in the Sixth are any better, or those in the Fourth and Third, or in the Seventh and Eighth. Good heavens! What a nomenclature! The city of New York is like a tall sum in addition, and the streets are like columns of figures" (654). Later, she will see the stoops "as ugly as a bad dream" (693), as earlier she has seen the sky over New York as seeming "part of the world at large; in Europe it's part of the particular place" (651). This echoes James's assertion in *Hawthorne* four years earlier that in the United States, in Hawthorne's day "there were no great things to look at (save forests and rivers)" (*EL* 383).

For the next twenty years and more, as he wrote increasingly about England and the English, James remained silent on the subject of New York. His bad dreams of the city seemed to be over. He had other places, Paris and Rome and Florence, to remember and note as they changed. But nothing in James's most complex personality was ever that simple.

The city of New York, in all its unresolved power, remained like an undertow in his consciousness for all the years. In 1906 in *The American Scene* he devoted three chapters to the city, having kept in reserve during his long exile a body of adjectives that he now hurled down on the teeming metropolis like a plague of locusts, so that his version of the city is closer to that of Kafka's *Amerika* than anything by Edith Wharton.

James begins by disliking New York harbor: "The shores are low and for the most part depressingly furnished and prosaically peopled; the islands, though numerous, have not a grace to exhibit" (*CTW* 417). He admits to "the beauty of light and air" (418), which is like admitting that the United States has forests and rivers to look at. Soon, however, James, using a peculiarly fervid tone, is writing about power, about which he was both uneasy and oddly thrilled:

> The aspect [of] power . . . is indescribable; it is the power of the most extravagant of cities, rejoicing, as with the voice of the morning, in its might, its fortune, its unsurpassable conditions, and imparting to every object and element, to the motion and expression of every floating, hurrying, panting thing, to the throb of ferries and tugs . . . something of its sharp free accent. . . . (418)

He wrote about "the bigness and bravery and insolence, specially, of everything that rushed and shrieked."

The city's skyscrapers strike him as

> impudently new and still more impudently "novel"—this in common with so many other terrible things in America—and they are triumphant payers of dividends. . . . Crowned not only with no history, but with no credible possibility of time for history, and consecrated by no uses save the commercial at any cost, they are simply the most piercing notes in that concert of the expensively provisional into which your supreme sense of New York resolves itself. (419–20)

It gets worse as James, visiting the business quarter, notes "the consummate monotonous commonness, of the pushing male crowd, moving in its dense mass" (425). He is appalled by the disappearance of some buildings and the dwarfing of others. He is, he admits, "haunted" by a "sense of dispossession" (427). He revisits his old city: "The precious stretch of space between Washington Square and Fourteenth Street had a value, had even a charm, for the revisiting spirit—a mild and melancholy glamour which I am conscious of the difficulty of 'rendering' for new and heedless generations" (428). The demolition of his birthplace at Washington Place had the effect, James writes, "of having been amputated of half my history" (431). He realizes that the very building that could have sported a tablet announcing the author's birthplace had been destroyed.

As he rails against the city, James finds astonishing images for the levels of distress he detects in the natives:

> Free existence and good manners, in New York, are too much brought down to a bare rigour of marginal relation to the endless electric coil, the monstrous chain that winds round the general neck and body, the general middle and legs, very much as the boa-constrictor winds round the group of the Laocoon. It struck me that when these folds are tightened in the terrible stricture of the snow-smothered months of the year, the New York predicament leaves far behind the anguish represented in the Vatican figures. (429)

Nothing pleases him. "This original sin," he writes,

> of the longitudinal avenues perpetually, yet meanly intersected, and of the organized sacrifice of the indicated alternative, the great perspectives from East to West, might still have earned forgiveness by some occasional departure from its pettifogging consistency. But, thanks to this consistency, the city is, of all great cities, the least endowed with any blest item of stately square or goodly garden, with any happy accident or surprise, any fortunate nook or casual corner, any deviation, in fine, into the liberal or the charming. (439)

Even the city's energy appalls him: "The very sign of its energy is that it doesn't believe in itself; it fails to succeed, even at a cost of millions, in persuading you that it does" (447).

James's horror of the new arrivals in the city and his use of animal imagery to evoke them make for some of the most uncomfortable reading in his entire opus. The immigrant in New York "resembles for the time the dog who sniffs round the freshly-acquired bone, giving it a push and a lick, betraying a sense of its possibilities, but not—and quite as from a positive deep tremor of consciousness—directly attacking it" (462). Of the Jewish population, he wrote:

> There are small strange animals, known to natural history, snakes or worms, I believe, who, when cut into pieces, wriggle away contentedly and live in the snippet as completely as in the whole. So the denizens of the New York Ghetto, heaped as thick as the splinters on the table of a glass-blower, had each, like the fine glass particle, his or her individual share of the whole hard glitter of Israel. (465)

The fire escapes, "[o]mnipresent in the 'poor' regions" (466) of the city, remind James "of the spaciously organized cage for the nimbler class of animals in some great zoological garden. This general analogy is irresistible—it seems to offer, in each district, a little world of bars and perches and swings for human squirrels and monkeys" (466–67). He watched, from a window in the Ghetto, "a swarming little square in which an ant-like population darted to and fro" (467).

It is hard to be precise about what exactly is biting Henry James as he wanders the streets of New York, this "terrible town," as he puts it (416), hating the voices and the accents he hears in the cafés, the "torture-rooms of the living idiom" (471), disliking even Central Park, comparing it "to an actress in a company destitute, through an epidemic or some other stress, of all other feminine talent; so that she assumes on successive nights the most dissimilar parts and ranges in the course of a week from the tragedy queen to the singing chambermaid" (501).

Something has been stolen from James, and it is not something ordinary. For certain writers, both places long abandoned and experiences just as well forgotten continue to exist in the present tense. They can be conjured up at will, and sometimes they come unwilled. They live lives of their own in the mind. They are like rooms whose electric lights cannot be dimmed or switched off. For James, the New York of 1848 to 1855 was such a place and his experiences there, so happy with the innocence of pre-puberty and full of ease, did not fade in his memory, as they may have done in his brother's memory. They remained living presences. He was moving now fifty years later in a city that tried, in name of novelty, to prevent him re-inhabiting his lighted rooms. James was not simply in the new city while remembering the old. The old city had never ended for him; it lived as an aspect of the imperative of his genius. Now the lights in his rooms were flickering madly, almost blinding him. To protect himself, he heaped insult upon insult on New York.

For a writer, the blurring of time present and time past is a way of freeing the imagination but also has a way of making one's personality both troubled and wilful. What he saw in 1905 in New York caused James to use imagery wildly disproportionate to his experience but apt for the battle going on within him between a past that clung to him and the terrible novelty of modernity. Writers die when they grow up; New York that year was asking James for too much.

It should be possible to argue, on the other hand, that the case was much simpler. James, it could be said, found more decent, human, and civilized values in the city of his childhood, genuinely disliked the city he found in 1905, and expressed himself robustly on the matter. But one of the last stories he wrote set in New York, and one of his last pieces of fiction, tends to favor the opposite argument, that there was something unresolved and haunting in James's dislike of New York and his fear of it. This story is called "The Jolly Corner."

James, like many of his contemporaries in London, was interested in doubles. His story "The Private Life," published in 1892, mirrored the world of Dorian Gray and Dr. Jekyll. In it, James dramatized his own life in society and company and his own vocation as a solitary man, a writer. He managed to place his writer in two places at exactly the same moment; he is both in company and alone at his desk. Now in early August 1906 James wrote to his agent, "I have an excellent little idea through not having slept a wink last night *all* for thinking of it, and must therefore at least get the advantage of striking while the iron is hot" (Edel, *Master* 320). In "The Jolly Corner," written after his American sojourn of 1905, James found a new doubled self to dramatize, the man who had left New York and lived in England and his double, still haunting him, who had never left, who still wandered in those same rooms that would fill James's autobiography and had filled *Washington Square*.

Spencer Brydon has been thirty-three years away from New York. He shares James's view of the city. Manhattan seems to him reduced "to some vast ledger-page, overgrown, fantastic, of ruled and criss-crossed lines and figures" (*CS3* 699). He sees his old friend Alice Staverton and muses on what a great man of business he might have become had he stayed in New York. Brydon has kept his old house downtown empty all the years, having it cleaned and cared for every day. He now goes there to be haunted by a figure moving in its dark rooms, the figure who has never left them, just as James himself in part of his mind has never left.

The men engage in the tussle throughout a long night, a battle to turn off the light in these rooms. "Rigid and conscious, spectral yet human, a man of his own substance and stature waited there to measure himself with his power to dismay" (724). Two fingers on the right hand that covers his face have been shot away. "The hands, as he looked, began to move, to open; then, as if deciding in a flash, dropped from the face and left it uncovered and presented. Horror, with the sight, had leaped into Brydon's throat, gasping there in a sound he couldn't utter" (725). "It is," Leon Edel has written, "a profoundly autobiographical tale" (*Master* 322). The story is a re-enactment of the battle that had taken place within James's own self as he returned to New York and set out to describe the world he saw, seeking in his descriptions to destroy the city, seeking to puncture its great power with the steel of his great paragraphs. He wanted to restore life to the world that lingered within him, the Old New York that he had experienced before the complications of puberty and unsettlement, that he had left when he was twelve. At the end of "The Jolly Corner," Brydon, who has come unscathed through his dark night with his double, is rescued by his old friend called Alice—James's sister-in-law and sister and the wife of his nephew were all called Alice. In the last sentence of "The Jolly Corner," he draws her to his breast. His reward for turning off the light has been a hint of love, the possibility of an uncomplicated sexuality as enjoyed by his brother William. "The Jolly Corner" leaves its protagonist stranded between a presexual past and an implausible present.

Two of the last stories James wrote were also set in the New York he had explored and deplored for *The American Scene*. The city as viewed in both "Crapy Cornelia" (1909) and "A Round of Visits" (1910) is almost sinister, quite vulgar, and deeply unsettling. Theodora Bosanquet, James's typist, to whom he dictated his fiction, noted on 17 December 1908: "Mr James going on with 'short' story for Harpers which extends mightily—& is, I think, dull" (Horne 470). Once more in "Crapy Cornelia" James is

working with an idea of a returned exile, a man who dislikes the new city
and remembers, with great nostalgia, the old. His protagonist notes the
house of Mrs. Worthingham in which "every particular expensive object
shriek[ed] at him in its artless pride" (*CS3* 821). He also makes what is
James's most eloquent attack on the lack of social cohesion in the city:
"This was clearly going to be the music of the future—that if people were
but rich enough and furnished enough and fed enough, exercised and
sanitated and manicured . . . all they had to do for civility was to take the
amused ironic view of those who might be less initiated" (829). He railed
against the lack of modesty in New Yorkers' display of their advantages:
"In *his* time . . . the best manners had been the best kindness, and the best
kindness had mostly been some art of not insisting on one's luxurious
differences, of concealing rather, for common humanity, if not for common decency, a part at least of the intensity or the ferocity with which one
might be 'in the know.' "

The city in "A Round of Visits," which was the last short story James
wrote, is even more inhospitable as Mark Monteith, another exile, returns
to New York, where he has been swindled by a New Yorker. As in "A Most
Extraordinary Case," written forty years earlier, the protagonist is ill in
a New York hotel. As in "An International Episode," written thirty years
earlier, the weather is impossible, this time "a blinding New York bliz-
zard," a "great white savage storm" (896). As in "Crapy Cornelia," the hero
goes to visit a number of old friends, deploring once more the interiors
of their houses with their "rather glaringly false accents" (910). What is
notable about these two stories is the deeply unsympathetic way in which
the New York women are presented. Edel has commented: "The women
particularly in these tales are devoid of all sympathy; fat and fatuous, ugly,
rich, cruel, they seem to have lost the meaning of kindness" (*Master* 506).
It is perhaps not surprising that the last moment of James's last New York
story involves a New Yorker blowing his brains out with a revolver.

"The Jolly Corner" was the single American tale that James allowed
into his twenty-three-volume New York Edition, from which he excluded
The Europeans, Washington Square, and *The Bostonians.* He worked on
the edition in the years between writing *The American Scene* and writing
his autobiography. In case there was any doubt that he meant business in

his battle to make his personal New York stand up to the Goliath daily rising on the island of Manhattan, he wrote to his publishers, Scribners, on 30 July 1905:

> If a *name* be wanted for the edition, for convenience and distinction, I should particularly like to call it the New York Edition if that may pass for a general title of sufficient dignity and distinctness. My feeling about the matter is that it refers the whole enterprise explicitly to my native city—to which I have had no great opportunity of rendering that sort of homage. (*HJL* 4: 368)

James's work would show to a world, much hardened against the idea, that the reverse of the picture, the soft side as he would call it, could endure and matter, could have a fame beyond money. The great house of fiction would stand as tall as any skyscraper, its rooms would remain well lit even as the world outside darkened.

WORKS BY HENRY JAMES

AU   *Autobiography*. Ed. Frederick W. Dupee. Princeton: Princeton UP, 1956.

CS1   *Complete Stories: 1864–1874*. New York: Library of America, 1999.

CS2   *Complete Stories: 1874–1884*. New York: Library of America, 1999.

CS3   *Complete Stories: 1898–1910*. New York: Library of America, 1996.

CT   *Complete Tales of Henry James*. Ed. Leon Edel. Vol. 1. Philadelphia: Lippincott, 1962.

CTW *Collected Travel Writings: Great Britain and America*. New York: Library of America, 1993.

EL   *Essays on Literature, American Writers, English Writers*. New York: Library of America, 1984. Vol. 1 of *Literary Criticism*.

HJL   *Henry James Letters*. Ed. Leon Edel. 4 vols. Cambridge: Belknap P of Harvard UP, 1974–1984.

NO   *Novels 1881–1886*. New York: Library of America, 1985.

PE   *The Painter's Eye*. Ed. John L. Sweeney. Cambridge: Harvard UP, 1989.

OTHER WORKS CITED

Buchan, John. *Memory Hold-the-Door*. Toronto: Musson, 1940.

Edel, Leon. *Henry James: The Conquest of London 1870–1881*. New York: Lippincott, 1962.

———. *Henry James: The Master 1901–1916*. New York: Lippincott, 1972.

———. *Henry James: The Untried Years 1843–1870*. New York: Lippincott, 1953.

Horne, Philip, ed. *Henry James: A Life in Letters*. New York: Viking, 1999.

CHAPTER SEVEN

A Death, a Book, an Apartment

The Portrait of a Lady

A specter haunted Henry James; it was the specter of George Eliot. He visited her first in 1869, when he was twenty-six, and wrote to his father:

> I was immensely impressed, interested and pleased. To begin with she is magnificently ugly—deliciously hideous. . . . Now in this vast ugliness resides a most powerful beauty which, in a few minutes steals forth and charms the mind, so that you end as I ended, in falling in love with her. Yes behold me literally in love with this great horse-faced blue-stocking. (*HJL* 1: 116)

Three years later, when *Middlemarch* appeared, James wrote from Rome to Grace Norton:

> a marvelous *mind* throbs in every page of *Middlemarch*. It raises the standard of what is to be expected of women—(by your leave!) We know all about the female heart; but apparently there is a female brain too. . . . To produce some little exemplary works of art is my narrow and lowly dream. They are to have less "brain" than *Middlemarch*; but (I boldly proclaim it) they are to have more *form*. (351)

James reviewed many of George Eliot's books at length, using a most serious tone, beginning with *Felix Holt* in 1866 and continuing with *The Spanish Gypsy* in 1868. In March 1873 his review of *Middlemarch* began: "'Middlemarch' is at once one of the strongest and one of the weakest of English novels" (*EL* 958), reflecting the view of his brother William, who had written to him a month earlier: "What a blasted artistic failure Middlemarch is but what a well of wisdom" (*WHJ* 90). Henry James's review includes the sentence: "It is not compact, doubtless; but when was a panorama compact?" (*EL* 959). And it is clear from his own subsequent prefaces to his books and from his letters that he did not wish to follow

George Eliot in writing "panorama" but that he did wish to follow her example in attempting to enter into the spirit of a single character, "[t]o render the expression of a soul" as he says of Eliot's Dorothea Brooke. "[W]e believe in her," he wrote, "as in a woman we might providentially meet some fine day. . . . By what unerring mechanism this effect is produced—whether by fine strokes or broad ones, by description or narration, we can hardly say; it is certainly the great achievement of the book" (*EL* 959–60).

As the 1870s went on, then, James began to imagine a creation of his own, a woman whom he might render in full, but in a novel that would be formally more pure than anything that George Eliot was capable of, a novel that would blend architectural perfection with unerring characterization. In 1878, he published "Daisy Miller," a tale of a spirited young American woman in Italy who was punished for breaking the rules, and also his tale called "An International Episode," in which another spirited young American woman was, to the surprise of her English friends, not in search of a rich husband, or any husband at all; she sought something more interesting from life than the mere prospect of money and rank.

His novel *The Portrait of a Lady* was, like *Roderick Hudson*, which was completed five years earlier, begun in Florence. James started writing it in the spring of 1879, and, like *Roderick Hudson* and *The American*, it was serialized in the *Atlantic Monthly* and also in London in *Macmillan's Magazine*. He continued working on the book the following year in Venice. When he came to write his preface to the book a quarter of a century later, he insisted that it did not come to him as plot "but altogether in the sense of a single character, the character and aspect of a particular engaging young woman" (*FW* 1071). He was alert as he wrote his preface to the idea that a young woman as the central subject of a work of art had to be defended, or at least explained. He appealed to the example of George Eliot, to her placing female characters such as Hetty Sorrel, Maggie Tulliver, Rosamond Vincy, and Gwendolen Harleth at the very center of her novels, remarking how difficult the task was, so difficult indeed that "Dickens and Walter Scott, as for instance even, in the main, so subtle a hand as that of R. L. Stevenson, has preferred to leave the task unattempted" (1077).

His decision, he wrote, was to "'place the centre of the subject in the young woman's consciousness.' . . . 'Stick to *that*—for the centre. . . . press least hard, in short, on the consciousness of your heroine's satellites, especially the male; make it an interest contributive only to the greater one'" (1079). He used imagery associated with architecture throughout in attempting to explain what he had in mind: "On one thing I was determined; that, though I should clearly have to pile brick upon brick for the creation of an interest, I would leave no pretext for saying that anything is out of line, scale or perspective" (1080). This meant, of course, that he would have to justify the undue amount of floor-space given in the early part of the book to Henrietta Stackpole, which he did very gracefully and disarmingly in his preface by acknowledging that he had "suffered Henrietta (of whom we have indubitably too much) so officiously, so strangely, so almost inexplicably, to pervade. . . . she exemplifies, I fear, in her superabundance, not an element of my plan, but only an excess of my zeal" (1083–84).

In creating Isabel, then, rather than trying to please his readers with the broad strokes—what he calls the "cultivation of the lively" (1085)—in which Henrietta was drawn, James was concerned with consciousness rather than plot. Nonetheless, he understood that a novel must have a body as well as a soul. Thus he asked in his preface: "What will she 'do'?" And his answer was: "Why, the first thing she'll do will be to come to Europe" (1083). And, he wrote, he "waked up one morning" in possession of those she would meet (1081). "I recognised them, I knew them, they were the numbered pieces of my puzzle, the concrete terms of my 'plot.'" Within the noise of this plot, he would place the power of silence, the slow and careful dramatization of an interior life, the silent registering of knowledge and experience, which, he wrote, for Isabel can throw "the action further forward than twenty 'incidents' might have done" (1084). In particular he mentioned the scene in which Isabel is alone by the dying fire as everything becomes clear. "[I]t all goes on without her being approached by another person and without her leaving her chair. It is obviously the best thing in the book" (1084).

James's language in his fiction was both mask and pure revelation; he played with the drama between circumlocution and bald statement. So, too, his prefaces were written both to reveal and to hide. While he was interested in describing his systems in creating form, he had a large interest in concealing where Isabel might have come from in his own past and how the people she would meet might have been there all along at the sharp edges of his memory, waiting patiently and firmly to enter his imagination unbeckoned.

In the second volume of his autobiography *Notes of a Son and Brother*, published in 1914 two years before his death, Henry James remembered the August of 1865 that he spent in North Conway with his cousin Minny Temple and her sisters, in the company of Oliver Wendell Holmes Junior and John Gray, both Civil War veterans, both to become distinguished lawyers. He wrote about

> the fraternizing, endlessly conversing group of us gather[ed] under the rustling pines. . . . the discussion of a hundred human and personal things, the sense of the splendid American summer drawn out to its last generosity. . . . in especial of my young orphaned cousins as mainly composing the maiden train and seeming as if they still had but yesterday brushed the morning dew of the dear old Albany naturalness." (*AU* 507–8)

He remembered his cousin Minny as being "beautifully and indescribably" a "heroine" (509, 508). "[E]verything that took place around her took place as if primarily in relation to her and in her interest: that is in the interest of drawing her out and displaying her the more. . . . She was absolutely afraid of nothing she might come to by living with enough sincerity and enough wonder" (509). He then went on to explain that within a few years it became clear that she was dying.

When he wrote about Minny's sincerity, her curiosity, her lightness touched with gravity, her charm, the play of her mind, her origins in Albany, her orphaned state, he could easily have been describing Isabel Archer. Soon after that summer in North Conway he began work on a story, "Poor Richard," his sixth to be published, in which a fascinating woman is surrounded and admired by three men, two of whom have fought in the Civil War, one of whom is ill. This story would have been, in its emotional contours, easy for Minny, Holmes, and Gray to recognize; it was a version of how they had spent the summer of 1865 with the author. In "Poor Richard," the heroine managed to marry none of the three and ended living in Florence.

So, too, when he came to write *The Portrait of a Lady* more than a decade later, he gave his lady three suitors, one of them also ill, and allowed her to turn down all three, each in a different way, so that in Florence, where he brought her to live, she would be able to exercise her considerable imagination with the help of a legacy from her aunt's husband. (The heroine of "Poor Richard" was also independently wealthy.) That summer in North Conway had given him, not exactly the idea for *The Portrait of a Lady*—idea is too strong a term—but a set of configurations that interested him, that held his imagination.

His cousin, who died in 1870, also held his imagination. She had adored the work of George Eliot. She harbored, she wrote to John Gray, an "overpowering admiration and affection for George Eliot" (qtd. in Gordon 94). She wrote to Henry James as she lay ill: "Have you seen Mrs. Lewes [George Eliot] yet? Kiss her for me—But, from all accounts, I don't believe that is exactly what one wish[es] to do to her" (100). Once Minny Temple was dead, James could conjure her up in his fiction without having to worry about her response. In a story "Travelling Companions," written soon after her death, he could imagine her in Italy, a country she had longed to visit. He could place her there once more in "Daisy Miller." Now he also sought to write an ambitious novel about her. "I had [Minny Temple] in mind," he wrote to Grace Norton as he worked on *Portrait*, "and there is in the heroine a considerable infusion of my impression of her remarkable nature" (*HJL* 2: 324). But in re-creating her as the central focus of a novel, in a large and well-proportioned house of fiction, James solved an interesting problem, one that he formulated first in a letter to his brother after her death. In life, he could not imagine Minny married, so free and original was her spirit. His portrait now could complete her, solve the puzzle of her. To Norton's suggestion that Isabel was a direct portrait: "Poor Minny was essentially *incomplete* and I have attempted to make my young woman more rounded, more finished."

In completing his heroine, writing the second half of his novel, offering his portrait a plot, James allowed his imagination to be nourished by two outside forces—one, a book, the other, an apartment. The book was George Eliot's *Daniel Deronda*; the apartment belonged to his friend Francis Boott, who lived with his daughter Lizzie above Florence in Bellosguardo.

Henry James wrote his first piece about *Daniel Deronda* in February 1876 when its first installment appeared in *Blackwood's Edinburgh Magazine*. At the end of that year, when the novel was published as a whole, he wrote an extraordinary second piece for the *Atlantic Monthly*. It was a long involved conversation between three people who had read the book. It was clear, from what they said, that James had, once more, problems with the form of the book and with many of its characters. But he allowed one of his own characters this observation of Gwendolen Harleth, the heroine: "Gwendolen is a masterpiece. She is known, felt and presented, psychologically, altogether in the grand manner" (*EL* 979). Her husband Grandcourt is "a consummate picture of English brutality."

James had in front of him then for his contemplation a novel that he viewed, as did his brother William, as a failure but whose central image of marital tyranny, pursued with such skill and brilliance by Eliot, could offer him an idea for his own novel. The drama surrounding the marriage of a passionate woman to a bully had appeared in scenes in other novels too, such as Trollope's *Phineas Finn* (1867), in which Lady Laura confesses to an unmarried man her deep unhappiness and sense of entrapment in marriage, much as Gwendolen does to Daniel Deronda, much as Isabel finally does to Ralph Touchett. James had merely to set about refining the passion, the bullying, the entrapment, the unhappiness, the confession, but he did not dilute them. Instead, by playing a game between what is unspoken and what is unspeakable, he made his drama more powerful.

Francis Boott, whom James had known in Boston, had reared his daughter Lizzie in Italy "as if she were a hot-house flower," as Leon Edel has written (110). In Florence, as he worked on his novel, James visited them very often in their apartment on Bellosguardo overlooking the city, using their relationship as bedrock for the relationship between Gilbert Osmond and his daughter Pansy and placing his fictional characters in the very rooms in which his friends lived, much as he had placed Isabel at the opening of the book in his own grandmother's house in Albany, also of course the house of Minny Temple's grandmother.

While James was in Florence working on the book, he saw a great deal as well of the American novelist Constance Fenimore Woolson, who had come with a letter of introduction to him. As Leon Edel has written: "[H]e turned on the full power of his charm for Miss Woolson" (411). She was to become one of his best friends, but as he worked on the book, it was enough for him that she was intelligent, deeply receptive to the sights of the city, and utterly American. Like most novelists, he used whatever came his way to deepen the texture of his novel. Osmond and Isabel would walk together in the places in Florence where he and Constance walked. When the book appeared, Constance wrote to him:

> With no character of yours have I ever felt myself so much in sympathy. . . . I found myself judging her and thinking of her with perfect . . . comprehension, and a complete acquaintance as it were; everything she did and said I judged from a personal standpoint. . . . I always knew exactly all about Isabel. . . . (qtd. in Gordon 167)

James used everything he knew, including his complex self, when he wrote *The Portrait of a Lady*. He dramatized his own interest in freedom against his own egotism, his own bright charm against the darker areas of his imagination. He also used the ghost of his cousin; he conjured up real houses; he described the cities of Rome and Florence that he had come to know and love; he wove in English manners, which he had, by the time he wrote the book, come to appreciate; and he allowed the books he had been reading, especially the novels of George Eliot, which placed a deeply intelligent and passionate woman at the center of a novel, to encourage him to make his young woman even more deeply intelligent and even more subtly passionate. He was fearless in his depiction of the play of her consciousness; her high ideals and her need for freedom are confronted with repression and dark restriction. In concentrating on her fate in the world, James created one of the most magnificent figures in the large and sprawling house of fiction.

WORKS BY HENRY JAMES

AU   *Autobiography*. Ed. Frederick W. Dupee. Princeton: Princeton UP, 1983.

EL   *Essays on Literature, American Writers, English Writers*. Ed. Leon Edel. New York: Library of America, 1984. Vol. 1 of *Literary Criticism*.

FW   *French Writers, Other European Writers, the Prefaces to the New York Edition*. Ed. Leon Edel. New York: Library of America, 1984. Vol. 2 of *Literary Criticism*.

HJL *Henry James Letters*. Ed. Leon Edel. 4 vols. Cambridge: Belknap P of Harvard UP, 1974–1984.

WHJ *William and Henry James: Selected Letters*. Ed. Ignas K. Skrupskelis and Elizabeth M. Berkeley. Charlottesville: U of Virginia P, 1997.

OTHER WORKS CITED

Edel, Leon. *Henry James: The Conquest of London*. New York: Lippincott, 1962.

Gordon, Lyndall. *A Private Life of Henry James: Two Women and His Art*. London: Chatto, 1998.

CHAPTER EIGHT

Reflective Biography

Review of Sheldon Novick. *Henry James: The Mature Master*. New York: Random, 2007.

On 23 January 1895, after the *Guy Domville* debacle, Henry James seemed to be determined that his failure in public would result in the creation of immortal work. He confided to his notebook: "I take up my *own* old pen again—the pen of all my old unforgettable efforts and sacred struggles. To myself—today—I need say no more. Large and full and high the future still opens. It is now indeed that I may do the work of my life. And I will" (*CN* 109).

In *Henry James: The Mature Master*, the second volume of his biography of James—the first *The Young Master* was published in 1997—Sheldon Novick notes what appeared next in James's notebooks. After a gap marked by a set of "x"s, James wrote: "I only have to *face* my problems." Then after more "x"s, he added: "But all that is of the ineffable—too deep and pure for any utterance. Shrouded in sacred silence let it rest." Then more "x"s.

What could James possibly have meant here? According to Novick, he is "using language that he reserved for personal relations too intimate to record even in his journal" (225). This is certainly one way of interpreting the journal entry. For anyone who reads, or reads into, James's later fiction and his letters after the mid-1890s, the idea that he had a secret and highly charged erotic life, real or even imaginary, is one of the lessons we might learn about the Master, one of the figures in the highly intricate carpet of his personality.

Novick, famously or notoriously, comes to the subject of James's secret sexuality with a history. In his first volume he looks carefully at the following passage in James's *Notebooks* and draws an interesting conclusion. The passage reads:

> The point for me (for fatal, for impossible expansion) is that I knew there, *had* there, in the ghostly old C[ambridge] . . . *l'initiation pre-mière* (the divine, the unique), there and in Ashburton Place. . . . Ah, the "epoch-making" weeks of the spring of 1865! . . . Something—some fine, superfine, supersubtle mystic breath of that may come in per-haps . . . Ah, that pathetic, heroic little *personal* prime of my own . . . of the unforgettable gropings and findings and sufferings and strivings and play of sensibility and of inward passion there. The hours, the moments, the days, come back to me . . . particular little thrills and throbs and daydreams there. (*CN* 238–39)

What could James be talking about? It seems to me that he is talk-ing about writing, about discovering a style and its attendant pleasures and remembering this discovery more than forty years later as pure sen-suality, in the same way as someone not a writer might remember first love, or sexual initiation. But I am not sure. James may indeed be writing about getting his rocks off for the first time in the only way he knew how to describe such things—obliquely, ambiguously, beautifully, and rather grandiloquently. And his partner may indeed, as Sheldon Novick has asserted, have been Oliver Wendell Holmes Junior, late of the Ameri-can Supreme Court. It is a marvelous idea and one for which Novick has taken his place as a controversial biographer of James.

In an introduction to a book of essays written in 1999, *Henry James and Homo-erotic Desire*, Novick wrote:

> As I have noted elsewhere, James left a series of hints in late remem-brances that the epochal bite of forbidden fruit was taken in company with the young Oliver Wendell Holmes. There is a good deal of indirect evidence . . . more [of which] will be included in the second volume of my biography—that this first bite of the apple was not an isolated incident, but was repeated with some regularity throughout his life; as I say, however, we don't have many details. Nor do we need them. The central point is the emotional reality of James's life, which is adequately on display in his letters and published works. (12)

What he is suggesting here is that James was not greatly troubled or puzzled by his own sexuality; its terms and conditions were clear. He was homosexual. The problem for biographers that then arises—and it will not go away—is how this sexuality manifested itself. Did James or did he not make love with some of his friends from early manhood or with some other blokes he met along the way, including servants and gondoliers, or with the younger men to whom he wrote with such affection in his later years? The answer is that he covered his tracks magnificently. Despite our best efforts to pretend that it doesn't matter, it matters enormously when we think about his life and even his art whether Henry James died a virgin or whether he took his pleasures when they offered themselves. He is a great mystery. As an artist, he played with ideas of secrecy with the possibility always of dramatic discovery. He may have really known as much about this as he seems to have imagined, and that was a great deal. Our interest in his private life is both prurient and pure.

In his new volume Novick takes James from 1881 and the publication of *The Portrait of a Lady* to his death in 1916; through the writing of his two quasi-political novels, *The Bostonians* and *The Princess Casamassima*; through his friendship with Robert Louis Stevenson; through his work in the theater; through his abandonment in the 1890s of the long novel for the short story, the short novel, and the novella; through his abandonment of London for Rye; through his creation in the early years of the twentieth century of his three late masterpieces, *The Ambassadors*, *The Wings of the Dove*, and *The Golden Bowl*; through his friendships with several young men and a few women; through his shifting relationship with his brother William and the death of his three other siblings; through his ill-health; and through his deep feelings of patriotism towards his adopted country as the First World War broke out.

In his preface and acknowledgments, Novick refers to the years between his own two volumes when "scholars have unearthed and made accessible a great mass of new material concerning the years of James's maturity, when he wrote the books for which he is now mainly remembered, that was not available to earlier biographers and from which I have greatly benefited" (ix). It should be said also that the appearances of Fred Kaplan's biography in 1992 and Novick's own first volume in 1997 were also important and ground breaking, full of fresh thinking and new insights. These studies, I think, meant that the brilliance of Lyndall Gordon's *A Private Life of Henry James: Two Women and His Art* (1998) and the significance of *Dearly Beloved Friends: Henry James's Letters to Younger Men*, edited by Susan E. Gunter and Steven H. Jobe (2001), could be more fully understood. The years between 1992 and 2001 changed how we saw James. For myself and for, I imagine, my colleague David Lodge—we both wrote novels about James—this meant that his personality became more complicated and interesting, more open to dramatization and interpretation.

Lyndall Gordon, who is, with Leon Edel, probably the most intelligent and perceptive interpreter James has ever had, if the most unforgiving, did not read James as a gay man in search of his destiny but as a selfish and determined artist feeding on the very experiences from which he was in flight. The value of her reading of his life lies in the sheer intelligence of her close analysis of James's relationship with two women—his cousin Minny Temple and his friend Constance Fenimore Woolson— and the nourishment he found in not only their lives but in their deaths. Novick does not deal much with the second of these relationships, with Woolson, which happens within the years of this volume of biography. It is strange—and disappointing—that he does not stitch the insights that Gordon has so stunningly made into his narrative and either argue with them or re-interpret them.

Novick *is* concerned, however, to re-interpret James as a less detached and less unhappy figure, less passive, less fearful and haunted and lonely than previous critical Henry Jameses. Here, James is an artist who takes life and friendship and artistic endeavor more in his stride than in other accounts of the life story.

Novick's James is, in certain ways, as with most subjects of a biographer, a strange reflection of the biographer himself. James as presented here is not quite as literal-minded as Novick, but at times it is a close-run race. When Novick says in his prologue that James wrote "frank love letters" to Hendrik Andersen (xviii) and adds soon afterwards that James's "only indisputable love letters were written to men" (13), the reader who knows these letters is entitled to feel that Novick's reading skills are not subtle. These letters can indeed be interpreted as love letters, but they can also be examples of an affectionate late style that gives more away than it intends. It might be best, in any case, to describe the letters carefully and judiciously in all their mixture of rotund ambiguity and flowery affection tinged with pure madness. They are many things, but they are not "frank" and they are not "indisputable." James was not given to frankness or indisputability. That is why we read him.

Novick, however, is capable of making distinctions of real interest. James's conquest of London, he makes clear, caused the novelist more grief than pleasure, not only because he had to go out every night in the season, which was a waste of his time, but because, as a mere writer, he was, in that world, nobody much. "In America," Novick writes, "he went in to dinner with the hostess or the most beautiful woman on his arm, but in London he came in at the tail end of the party and was seated with no one in particular" (10). This meant that, for a man so interested in status and power, living in the largest house in Rye was a rich reward for his labors rather than an effort to be quiet and retired and away from the noise of London. I wish I had thought of that when I was writing my novel.

Novick also convincingly and emphatically places James in a milieu with which we do not normally associate him—bachelors who were either obviously or opaquely homosexual—and makes clear how relaxed James was in this world and how much he was capable of cavorting with the best of them.

Novick, like many biographers who are good and decent people, would like his subject to be good and decent too, causing this reader, at times, to laugh out loud. He seems to feel that it might have been better had James taken part in some contemporary version of the Stonewall riots and the March on Washington. He writes, for example:

> In *The Tragic Muse* he gave what now seems an all-but-explicit and negative portrayal of an openly gay man. This latter has been particularly puzzling, because James's own loves were, so far as is known, exclusively male. . . . Here and elsewhere, James seems to accept the conventional view that homosexual love is essentially immature and irresponsible. There is certainly a problem here. . . . James's acceptance of conventional roles and stereotypes of race and gender, his belief in their essential truth, is distasteful. (140)

On James's refusal to sign a petition for Oscar Wilde, Novick writes: "Surely there would have been some intrinsic value in a protest?" (245). When Arthur Benson did not, at one point, join James in Rye, Novick writes: "once again James had missed the chance for settled intimacy" (319). It is hard not to feel that Novick, who is clearly a very nice man, is out of his depth in writing about James. His next book should be about someone good and holy.

Sometimes it is also hard to know what Novick means but easy to see what he is hinting at. He seems to be suggesting, for example, that James and his one-time agent Wolcott Balestier were lovers by writing, "The few summer days they now spent on the Isle of Wight marked a deepening of their intimate friendship. Alice wrote in her diary, after that summer, that she hoped Balestier would be a lifelong companion, as well as a business friend, for James" (168). There is something odd and disingenuous about the word "intimate" here, and the reference to Alice's diary is not quite straightforward. Alice wrote in her diary immediately after she had heard the news of Balestier's early death and not just "after that summer" (although it was also, of course, after that summer), and what she wrote should be read in that context (223). In a final sentence to a chapter on James and Hendrik Andersen, Novick writes: "Visit would follow visit, and Andersen would be a most intimate friend" (305). Does he mean here what I think he means?

In his introductory essay to *Henry James and Homo-erotic Desire*, Novick states of Arthur Benson's diaries and his relationship to James: "The diary entries and the letters suggest that this was most likely a chaste if romantic friendship" (5). But in his biography, Novick seems more coy on the subject of Benson:

> Arthur did come to dinner one Saturday during his school holidays, and although he had Lambeth Palace at his disposal during his visits to London, he stayed overnight and remained until Monday at De Vere Gardens [where James lived], where, as James assured him would be the case, no one else was in the house but the servants and Tosca [the dog]. It was the first of many overnight visits and marked a new stage of intimacy in their relations. (246)

(Come on, Sheldon, you can spell it out! There is only one direction here in which we are being nudged, and its final destination is that the intimacy you are writing about was sexual intimacy. You can say it, come on, don't be afraid!)

Three pages later, Novick is at it again as he observes about the circle of young men to whom James wrote letters, the guys whom he saw generally: "In the midst of his struggle to establish himself on a new footing, professionally and financially, the only affection he seemed to return vigorously and passionately was Arthur Benson's" (249). Vigorously and passionately? I think I get the point.

Every writer on James since 1920, when some of his letters to younger men were first published, has had to deal with how to read them. Novick quotes from a letter where James is "panting" to see Benson and thus was "taken up with living in the future and in the idea of answering you with impassioned lips" (qtd. in Novick 249). Novick goes on to quote him writing to Benson after their holiday visits: "if I can pick your bones before the last scrap of you—and of me—is gobbled up, I suppose I shall be entitled to say that I have known friendship and intimacy in what they have of most intense and abandoned. *Pazienza*. . . . Consign to no deadlier limbo than you can help, the pale phantom of our intercourse" (249).

Novick then writes:

> Although the conventions of the day allowed what later would seem to be startling expressions of affection between men, James's references to "impassioned lips," to "intense and abandoned intimacy," his later invitation to make an overnight visit in which he promised to embrace and enfold his visitor were well out of the ordinary. A minimum of discretion was observed, he wrote in double entendres, but he was reassuring Benson of his love and his language could hardly be misunderstood. (249–50)

It seems to me, on the other hand, that his language could be easily misunderstood. And if James were actually having sex with Benson— Novick never states this as fact although clearly leading us to think it— then James would be unlikely in an age of the blackmailer, with Wilde still serving his sentence, to write to Benson at all or in any way except the most chaste and careful. The language of these letters, in fact, seems to point to James's effusive innocence. The fact that he did not take greater care in the terms he used suggests that there was no reason why he should have. He delighted in metaphorical and ambiguous language, and he had fun writing these letters. The recipients must have been amazed and, at times, embarrassed by them. But James was not a fool; the letters were, it seems to me, proof of nothing concrete that could have been used in evidence against him.

Nonetheless, it has to be said, some of them are absolutely extraordinary, all the more so when we read the ones dictated to Theodora Bosanquet, James's secretary, which Novick quotes. To Walter Berry, for example: "You are victor, winner, master, Oh Irresistible One—you've done it, you've brought it off and got me down forever and I must just feel your weight and bear your might" (qtd. in Novick 493). Perhaps the most interesting piece of information in this entire book is the news that James added a postscript in his own handwriting to this letter, which Berry, who kept all James's letters, tore off and destroyed.

One could argue forever with Novick over his strenuous efforts to make sense of this strange and brilliant life. It also has to be said, however, that, while he is not a literary critic or a stylist himself, this second volume of his biography is a serious and respectful contribution to our understanding of James. Novick admires the late novels and adds to our comprehension of James's work in the theater. It may be a sign of my age and provincial background that I still love and trust Leon Edel's five-volume biography of James, but this book, despite my problems with its detail, seeks with integrity and insight to interpret the Master as less long-suffering and much stronger and happier than we might previously have imagined. Novick's James slept easy in his bed, at least most of the time, and we can sleep easier too, consoled by this fact, even if we do not quite believe it.

WORKS BY HENRY JAMES

CN   *The Complete Notebooks of Henry James*. Ed. Leon Edel and Lyall H. Powers. New York: Oxford UP, 1987.

OTHER WORKS CITED

Gordon, Lyndall. *A Private Life of Henry James: Two Women and His Art*. New York: Norton, 1998.

James, Alice. *The Diary of Alice James*. Ed. Leon Edel. New York: Dodd, 1964.

Jobe, Steven H., and Susan Gunther, eds. *Dearly Beloved Friends: Henry James's Letters to Younger Men*. Ann Arbor: U of Michigan P, 2002.

Kaplan, Fred. *Henry James: The Imagination of Genius*. New York: Morrow, 1992.

Novick, Sheldon. "Introduction." *Henry James and Homo-Erotic Desire*. Ed. John R. Bradley. Palgrave Macmillan, 1999. 1–24.

———. *Henry James: The Mature Master*. New York: Random, 2007.

———. *Henry James: The Young Master*. New York: Random, 1996.

CHAPTER NINE

A Bundle of Letters

Review of *The Complete Letters of Henry James, 1855–1872*. Ed. Pierre A. Walker and Greg W. Zacharias. 2 vols. Lincoln: U of Nebraska P, 2006.

After the death of Henry James's father in 1882, his sister-in-law Catharine Walsh, better known as Aunt Kate, burned a large collection of family papers, including many letters between Henry James Senior and his wife. Henry James himself in later life made a number of bonfires in which he destroyed a great quantity of the letters he had received. He often added an instruction to letters he himself wrote: "Burn this!" (To one correspondent, he wrote: "burn my letter with fire or candle [if you have *either*! Otherwise, wade out into the sea with it and soak the ink out of it]" [*HJL* 4: 436].) In two of his stories, "The Aspern Papers" and "Sir Dominick Ferrand," valued letters are turned to illegible ashes "as a kind of act of sadism on posterity," in the words of Leon Edel (*HJL* 1: xiii). James was fully alert to the power of letters, having paid close attention to the published correspondence of Balzac, Flaubert, and George Sand, and, indeed, the power of editors when he read Sidney Colvin's edition of the letters of his friend Robert Louis Stevenson. ("One has the vague sense of omissions," he wrote. "[O]ne *smells* the thing unprinted" [xxxiii].)

In the years after James's death, his family in the United States was concerned about his reputation, especially about what Edel called their "uncle's relaxed homoerotism" (xxiii); thus they refused Hendrik Andersen, whom, as Edel put it, James "loved in so troubled a way," the right to publish James's letters to him, and these have only appeared in recent years in a bilingual Italian edition, *Amato Ragazzo* (2000), edited by Rosella Mamoli Zorzi and in *Letters to Younger Men* (2002), edited by Susan Gunter and Steven Jobe.

The first letters of James to be published came in two volumes, containing 403 letters, edited by Percy Lubbock, and overseen by the James family, in 1920, just four years after the novelist's death. In dealing with the family, Lubbock found Mrs. William James, the formidable widow of Henry James's elder brother, moving "in a cloud of fine discretions and hesitations and precautions" (qtd. in *HJL* 1: xviii). James's sister-in-law, for example, disliked Edith Wharton "thoroughly—and morbidly" as Edel put it (xvii), and this meant that Wharton or anyone else deemed disreputable could not be involved in any aspect of the estate. Theodora Bosanquet, James's deeply intelligent final amanuensis, thought that this was a pity and recorded in her diary that Lubbock "joined me in a regret that Mrs. Wharton hadn't been left in charge. He feels it's awfully difficult to offer advice to people like the Jameses, and yet they do need some very badly!" (92). The text of Lubbock's two volumes was gone over by three of William James's children and by their mother. "The family scrutiny was thorough," Edel wrote (*HJL* 1: xxi).

As the children of William James, they had been brought up by their father to believe that their Uncle Henry in England was slightly silly, but now, as Harry James, son of William, read these letters he was deeply impressed at their tone and their gravity. He wrote to his sister Peggy:

> It will, I rather think, make Uncle Henry count very much more than he did already. For it's full of literature as well as character. In fact I suspect that these letters will become, in the history of English literature, not only one of the half dozen greatest epistolary classics, but a sort of milestone—the last stone of the age whose close the Great War has marked. They are a magnificent commentary on the literary life of his generation, and they're done in a style which will never be used naturally again. (qtd. in *HJL* 1: xxvii)

In the years that followed, Harry James was contacted by many people who had bundles of letters from his uncle. Having allowed two slim volumes of these to appear, both of which he then came to dislike, he was hesitant thereafter to grant permission for any more such volumes. Even as late as 1955, when Leon Edel, who also wrote a five-volume biography of James, edited a *Selected Letters*, his work was still overseen by the family. "I remember removing a letter dealing with *Guy Domville* from the *Selected Letters*," Edel wrote, "because Billy James [another nephew] found 'it too sad'" (*HJL* 1: xxxiv). Between 1974 and 1984 Edel published his four-volume edition with 1,100 letters, noting that "the large James archives in many libraries will provide opportunities for amplification and further collections in the years to come" (xxxvi).

In 1999 when Philip Horne edited *Henry James: A Life in Letters*, which remains the best single selection of James's letters—the greatest hits, all 296 of them, superbly annotated and put in context—he pointed out that half of the letters he had included had not been published before. He estimated that there are between 12,000 and 15,000 letters by James in existence and suggested that James may have written many more that may be still in private hands. (Horne, in fact, calculated that James may have written as many as 40,000 letters in his lifetime, many of them now lost.) Some further unpublished letters had by then appeared in other editions, notably a single volume of letters between Henry and his brother William and another single volume of letters between Henry and Edith Wharton. Steven Jobe in his *Partial Calendar of James Letters*, updated in 1994, listed the letters that he could locate, making clear that a good number of them were to be found scattered in more than 200 books and journals and the originals in 132 repositories and private collections.

It was obvious that a collected edition of James's letters was needed. The project was first discussed by scholars in the early 1990s. This was made easier by the fact that, as the editors of *The Complete Letters of Henry James* have stated in their "General Introduction" to Volume 1,

> Leon Edel was at the very end of his career and exerted far less control over access to and publication permission for Henry James's letters than he had when he was younger. The executorship of the James papers had been passed from Alexander R. James to his daughter, Bay James, following Alexander James's death. Whereas some of her predecessors, at times at Edel's urging, had limited full access to and publication permission for Henry James's letters, Bay James encouraged open access and full permission. (*CL* 1: xlix–l)

These two volumes, which cover James's correspondence from his earliest known letter through to 1872, when he was twenty-nine, contain 161 letters, of which fifty-two are published for the first time. The final edition of the letters—10,423 of which are in the editors' hands, but more are expected to come to light—will be in more than 140 volumes.

These two volumes are dominated by the James family's European wanderings and then by Henry James's first visit alone to Europe, especially his travels in England and Italy. They throw much light on his relationship with his family and his country of birth while at the same time helping us towards some understanding of his health problems, such as they were. Some of the letters from Italy are small masterpieces of description; they are alert and sensitive and full of astute judgments. Sometimes also James is very funny, irreverent, and outspoken, especially in his letters to his family but also those to literary friends from Newport and Boston such as Thomas Sergeant Perry and Charles Eliot Norton.

To Norton on Germans, for example: "Such men—such women—such children! . . . Even the comparatively good-looking ones suffer from the ugliness of the others & are injured by the hideous contagion" (*CL* 2: 47). To his brother William on Venetians:

> In the narrow streets the people are far too squalid & offensive to the nostrils, but with a good breadth of canal to set them off and a heavy stream of sunshine to light them up, as they go pushing & paddling & screaming—bare-chested, bare-legged, magnificently tanned & muscular—the men at least are a very effective lot. (119)

To his sister Alice on Pope Pius IX: "When you have seen that flaccid old woman waving his ridiculous fingers over the prostrate multitude & have duly felt the picturesqueness of the scene—& then turn away sickened by its absolute *obscenity*—you may climb the steps of the Capitol & contemplate the equestrian statue of Marcus Aurelius" (175). To his father on the Pope: "When the Pope, clad in shining robes crept up to the altar & in the midst of that dazzling shrine of light, possessed himself of the Host & raised it aloft over the prostrate multitudes, I got a very good look at him by poking up my head & confronting that terrible toy" (226). To Alice on the view from St. Peter's in Rome: "I'm sure I saw one of the pontifical petticoats hanging out to dry" (178). To William on the Italian past: "I conceived at Naples a tenfold deeper loathing than ever of the hideous heritage of the past—& felt for a moment as if I should like to devote my life to laying rail-roads & erecting blocks of stores on the most classic & romantic sites" (241). To William on the women in Malvern: "I am tired of their plainness & stiffness & tastelessness—their dowdy heads, their dirty collars & their linsey woolsey trains" (314).

These letters were written before James developed his views on the thinness of the American experience, before his attempts to justify his own exile in England, before his efforts over many years to soak up, for the sake of his fiction, the atmosphere in France and Italy. In 1860 at the age of seventeen, for example, he wrote from Bonn to Thomas Sergeant Perry in the sort of patriotic tones that he would more than forty years later satirize in *The Ambassadors*: "I think that if we are to live in America it is about time we boys should take up our abode there; the more I see of this estrangement of American youngsters from the land of their birth, the less I believe in it. It should also be the land of their breeding" (*CL* 1: 47). Seven years later he wrote again to Perry: "One feels—I feel at least, that he [Sainte-Beuve] is a man of the past, of a dead generation; and that we young Americans are (without cant) men of the future. . . . We are Americans born—*il faut en prendre son parti*. I look upon it as a great blessing; and I think that to be an American is an excellent preparation for culture" (179). Five years later, he wrote to Charles Eliot Norton: "I exaggerate the merits of Europe. It's the same world there after all & Italy isn't the absolute any more than Massachusetts. It's a complex fate, being an American, & one of the responsibilities it entails is fighting against a superstitious valuation of Europe" (2: 438).

His valuation of Europe may have ended as an artistic one, but its allure, at least in these early years, was much simpler: it was a beautiful way of getting away from his family. These letters make clear, more than anything, how necessary that was, and how difficult. Despite his father's interest in his schooling, it was obvious to him, even at the age of sixteen, that he was not being prepared for a profession, or for anything much at all. He wrote to Perry from Geneva: "The School is intended for preparing such boys as wish to be engineers, architects, machinists, 'and the like' for other higher schools, and I am the only one who is not destined for either of the useful art[s] or sciences, although I am I hope for the art of being useful in some way" (1: 18). The following year he wrote to Perry from Bonn about the family's return to Newport: "I have not the remotest idea of how I shall spend my time next winter. . . . I wish, although I've no doubt it is a very silly wish, that I were going to college" (62).

His problem was that he had nothing to do. This led to intense periods of reading and writing, but it also led to his needing an alibi as he grew into his twenties, something with which he could justify himself and which would also match his parents' needs. His famous bad back perhaps arose from a malady more serious than an actual physical injury, the malady of being a member of the James family with no escape route. By 1867, the question of James's back and other mysterious illnesses were appearing with regularity in his letters, slowly becoming an excuse for him to be sent to Europe—or at least somewhere else. In November, for example, he wrote to William from the family home in Cambridge:

> It is plain that I shall have a very long row to hoe before I am fit for anything—for either work or play. . . . An important element in my recovery, I believe, is to strike a happy medium between reading &c, & social relaxation[]. The latter is not to be obtained in Cambridge—or only a ghastly simulacrum of it. There are no "distractions" here. (1: 189)

Once in Europe, he made sure to pepper each letter home with accounts of the state of his condition, some of them very vague indeed. From London in March 1869 he wrote to his sister: "There is no sudden change, no magic alleviation; but a gradual & orderly recurrence of certain phenomena which betray the slow development of such soundness as may ultimately be my earthly lot" (240). To William soon afterwards, he wrote: "I feel every day less & less fatigue. I made these long recitals of my adventures in my former letters only that you might appreciate how much I am able to do with impunity . . . I mentioned all the people & things I saw, without speaking of the corresponding intervals of rest, which of course have been numerous & salutary" (247–48). From Malvern a month later, he wrote to William again: "The place is unfortunately built up & down hill & whenever one goes out it is always (in some degree) a perpendicular trudge—which for a man with my trouble is a circumstance to be regretted" (274).

In this letter James made clear what one of the problems really was, having hinted at it in an early letter to his mother. He was plagued with constipation. However, things began to improve; he told William that he "had a movement every day for a month—& at Oxford *two* daily" (317). But as soon as he reached the Continent, things grew worse. From Florence he wrote in October: "I may actually say that *I can't get a passage.* My 'little squirt' has ceased to have more than a nominal use. The water either remains altogether or comes out as innocent as it entered" (2: 136). Pills he took did not help, he wrote again; instead they brought "a species of abortive diarrhea. That is I felt the most reiterated & most violent inclination to stool, without being able to effect anything save the passage of a little blood" (149). He saw a doctor who "examined them [his bowels] (as far as he could) by the insertion of his finger (horrid tale!) & says there is no palpable obstruction. He seemed surprised however that I haven't piles; you see we always have something to be grateful for" (150). At the end of the letter, he wrote: "Having opened up the subject at such a rate, I shall of course keep you informed.—To shew you haven't taken this too ill, for heaven's sake make me a letter about your own health—poor modest flower!" (153).

At this stage Henry James was twenty-six and his brother less than two years older. They would both live to be reasonably old, remaining vigorous, active, and healthy most of their lives, dying eventually from the same type of heart disease. In April that same year in a letter from Malvern, Henry James wrote to William: "Of course I have been sorry to think that you have been unable to write before by reason of your back & have greatly missed hearing from you" (1: 273). Illness within the James family was like money in some families or worldly success or religious devotion in others. It was discussed in hushed and reverent tones, and those who did not benefit from it won no brownie points. William and Henry were lucky; they knew how far to go with it, how to refer to it enough but not too much; they understood how much to invent and how much to make of what was real. Unfortunately, their sister Alice, who all her life made illness into a mysterious fine art, knew simply that she would need to be ill to survive her father's erratic, chattering presence and her mother's suffocating and controlling care, but she did not know how to stop it when it was not necessary in the same way as her two eldest brothers did.

Thus Henry James's constipation would be described by himself in detail as well as his position as someone who, because of his back, "shall certainly never get beyond having to be minutely cautious" (*CL* 2: 54). When William wanted to get nasty, as he often did, it was Henry's back he went for. In June 1869, for example, he wrote to him: "The condition of your back is totally incomprehensible to me" (*WHJ* 45). But Henry managed always to dramatize his plight, mentioning on his return to Malvern symptoms as "powerful testimony to the obstinacy of my case" and later to his "invalidism," his "slowly crawling from weakness & inaction & suffering into strength & health & hope" (*CL* 2: 312, 342). When Henry's general condition seemed to get worse at one point in his European sojourn, he wrote to his father about himself as though he were translating from the heightened language of a Greek tragedy: "Don't revile me & above all don't pity me. . . . Dear father, if once I can get rid of this ancient sorrow I shall be many parts of a well man" (*CL* 2: 161).

He ended his letter by suggesting that there was a family pool of illness, or a see-saw on which they all sat waiting their turn on top. "I have invented for my comfort a theory that this degenerescence of mine is the [the word 'the' is then crossed out] a result of Alice & Willy getting better & locating some of their diseases on me—so as to propitiate the fates by not turning the poor homeless infirmities out of the family. Isn't it so? I forgive them & bless them" (161–62).

He did not stop. In letter after letter to his parents, to his brother William and his sister Alice he remembered to mention the poor state of his health. He even tried it out on his friend Grace Norton, the sister of Charles Eliot Norton. Sometimes when he has been giving breathless descriptions of places seen and excursions made you realize that he thinks he had best mention it soon or they will send for him or stop believing him. In some cases, the claim to illness reads like an afterthought, other times, an excuse. When he was accused of spending too much money, for example, Henry wrote: "My being unwell has kept me constantly from attempting in any degree to rough it" (281). When he wished to travel further, spending even more money, it was his health he mentioned as his motive. From London he wrote to his father attempting to justify his urge to travel after taking the waters at Malvern:

> When I left Malvern, I found myself so exacerbated by immobility & confinement that I felt it to be absolutely due to myself to test

the impression which had been maturing in my mind, that a certain amount of regular lively travel would do me more good than any further treatment or further repose. . . . I have now an impression amounting almost to a conviction that if I were to travel steadily for a year I would be a good part of a well man. (1: 309)

And in case that was not enough, he had to make them believe that he missed them. From London in March 1869 he wrote: "What is the good of having a mother—& such a mother—unless to blurt óut to her your passing follies & miseries? . . . Yes—I confess it without stint or shame—I am homesick—abjectly, fatally homesick" (224). He mentioned how sad he was not to be "lolling on that Quincy St. [where the Jameses lived] sofa, in consequence—with my head on mother's lap & my feet in Alice's!" (225). But by the end of the letter, to forestall the suggestion that he should come home now as a way of curing his homesickness, he cheerfully announced, "Cancel, dearest mother, all the maudlinity of the beginning of my letter; the fit is over; the ghost is laid . . . I assure you I shall do very well" (230). From Geneva in the same year the twenty-six-year-old tried it on again: "I feel my weekly palpitations at letter-time. I assure you dearest mother, they are violent. I am chronically, desperately, mournfully, shamelessly homesick" (2: 7).

Henry James's letters home can be read as sly and manipulative, but he wrote them for a good reason. He had been haphazardly educated by his parents to prepare him for nothing; they had kept him away from America for some of the crucial years of his adolescence so that his circle of friends, as these letters show, was extremely limited, many of his associates being also friends of the family. His parents had effectively banished their two younger sons, Wilkie and Bob, in whom they never had any great interest. They had made Alice, their only daughter, an invalid. And one evening in 1876 their father came home from an outing to announce that he had met the woman whom his son William would marry, whose name was also Alice. William duly married her. (Forty years later she became that same widow who disapproved of Edith Wharton.) In other words, the parents of Henry James had to be watched very carefully. Escaping them was an imperative. If illness, real or imaginary, kept them at bay, distracted them from doing damage, then it was a small price to pay. Had Henry James not managed them so cleverly, he might never have gotten away from them. Or have managed the parting with such ease, such a lack of rancour, making clear to them—once he had left for good—that he loved them and missed them and basked in the glow of their love and approval, but from afar.

Managing his family with slow doses of deceit was also useful to James as a novelist for whom secrecy and subterfuge was a great theme, the foundation on which his best novels were built. Manipulating others, bending them with subtlety toward one's will, sweetly deceiving them, was something his characters would do with considerable skill. At times, as with Chad in *The Ambassadors*, it would be done with something approaching innocence; other times, as with Madame Merle in *The Portrait of a Lady* or Kate Croy in *The Wings of the Dove*, it would be done out of dark need; finally, as with Maggie Verver in *The Golden Bowl*, it would be done with such aplomb and so stylishly that no one was sure they had noticed.

In this first visit alone to Europe, which began in February 1869 and ended in April 1870, James saw a great deal. Many of his visits to painters and writers were set up for him by Charles Eliot Norton, sixteen years his senior, who had published his early reviews in the *North American Review* and was one of the founders of the *Nation*. Norton and his family were also in Europe at the time of James's visit. (Some of James's most stilted and insufferable letters in these two volumes were written to members of the Norton family.) With the Nortons in London, James saw Leslie Stephen, whom James's father had also known, and met Charles Dickens's daughter, who was, he reported to Alice, "plain-faced, ladylike (in black silk & black lace)" (1: 236), and visited William Morris and his family. Mrs. Morris, he wrote, was "[a] figure cut out of a missal. . . . It's hard to say whether she's a grand synthesis of all the pre-Raphaelite pictures ever made—or they a 'keen analysis' of her—whether she's original or a copy. In either case she is a wonder" (237). With Charles Norton he visited Ruskin's house and saw his paintings and later, with the Nortons (Charles Eliot Norton's sister-in-law, Sara Sedgwick, would later marry Darwin's son), saw Charles Darwin. "Darwin," he wrote to his father, "is the sweetest, simplest, gentlest old Englishman, you ever saw. . . . He said nothing wonderful & was wonderful in no way but in not being so" (263).

Soon before he left England in May 1869, James went with Sara Sedgwick and Grace Norton to see George Eliot. James tried to list her characteristics: "a broad hint of a great underlying world of reserve, knowledge, pride & power—a great feminine dignity & character in these massively plain features—a hundred conflicting shades of consciousness & simpleness—shyness & frankness—graciousness & remote indifference—these are some of the more definite elements of her personality" (311).

After much procrastination in Switzerland, James finally made his way into Italy at the end of August 1869, noting "the delight of seeing the north slowly melt into the south" (2: 83), unaware of what a momentous occasion this small step over the border that summer was for the novels he would write. This sense of Henry James wandering innocently and voraciously, not knowing as he moved how important some of these places would become for both him and his readers, makes these pages thrilling and fascinating. It is hard not to shiver when he writes to his mother in November from Rome of his visit to "that divine little protestant Cemetery where Shelley & Keats lie buried—a place most lovely & solemn & exquisitely full of the traditional Roman quality—with the vast grey pyramid inserted into the sky on one side & the dark cold cypresses on the other & the light bursting out between them & the whole surrounding landscape swooning away for very picturesqueness" (2: 208).

Nine years later he would bury his character Daisy Miller in this graveyard by "an angle of the wall of imperial Rome, beneath the cypresses and the thick spring-flowers" (CS 72). By the end of the century he would often find himself standing in the cemetery at the grave of his friend Constance Fenimore Woolson, who committed suicide in Venice in 1894, close to the graves of the sculptor William Wetmore Story, about whom he would write a book, and John Addington Symonds, on whom he would base his story "The Author of Beltraffio."

In this first visit to Italy he was stepping lightly on places he and his characters would subsequently grow to know intimately, to suffer in, to haunt. He studied churches and pictures and pieces of sculpture with enormous care. There is a constant impression in these months of his eye feasting on things, his sensibility sharpened and refined by travel and solitude; he is ready to make sweeping, confident, discriminating judgments for the benefit of the folks at home. Some of these letters with their tone of pure youthful delight have a greater urgency and fluency than the

essays in his book *Italian Hours*. At the end of 1869, for example, he wrote
to William about the Raphaels he had been seeing in Rome:

> There was in him none but the very smallest Michael Angelesque
> elements—I fancy that I have found after much fumbling & worry-
> ing . . . the secret of his incontestable thinness & weakness. He was
> incapable of energy of statement. . . . this energy—positiveness—cour-
> age—call it what you will—is a simple fundamental primordial qual-
> ity in the supremely superior genius. . . . I felt this morning irresistibly
> how that M. Angelo's greatness lay above all in the fact that he *was*
> this man of action—the greatest almost, considering the temptation he
> had to be otherwise—considering how his imagination embarrassed &
> charmed & bewildered him—the greatest perhaps, I say, that the race
> has produced. (*CL* 2: 239–40)

James spent most of his time in Italy alone. It is possible that these
months contemplating great monuments and looking at paintings in detail
marked a crucial change in his ambitions. This tour was not merely about
getting away from his family or tackling his so-called health problems;
it also offered him a much grander and richer scenario than had come
his way among his Boston associates. Michelangelo's "high transcendent
spirit" (240) rescued James from the limited universe of the Jameses, the
Nortons, and the Sedgwicks, the dull world of Boston letters. When, two
years after his return from Europe, his brother William and some of his
friends in Boston founded a club, James wrote to Charles Eliot Norton:
"my brother & various other long-headed youths have combined to form
a metaphysical club, where they wrangle grimly & stick to the question. It
gives me a headache just to know of it" (2: 438). A few months earlier he
had written to Norton about his friend William Dean Howells:

> His talent grows constantly in fineness, but hardly, I think, in range of
> application. I remember your saying some time ago that in a couple of
> years when he had read Ste. Beuve &c, he would come to his best. But
> the trouble is he will never read Ste. Beuve, nor care to. He has little
> intellectual curiosity; so here he stands with his admirable organ of
> style, like a poor man holding a diamond & wondering how he can
> wear it. It's rather sad, I think, to see Americans of the younger sort

so unconscious and unambitious of the commission to do the *best*.
(414–15)

As James wrote these letters from his parents' house in Boston it was clear that he could not stay for much longer in the city where ambitions were limited and young intellectuals stuck to the question. Within three years he would be gone for good.

James did not find his immediate family interesting enough to use them much as models in his fiction; it is possible to find traces of Alice in *The Bostonians* and *The Princess Casamassima*, but of William hardly anything. William Dean Howells's unworn diamond did become useful when James needed an American character for *The Ambassadors* whose sensuous nature had been stifled by America to be woken by the glory of Paris when it was too late. By the time he left America, James's knowledge of its society was deeply limited and seriously etiolated. This lack of deep roots was an enormous help, a great gift to him in his fiction; it forced him to concentrate on character and style and saved him from writing dull novels about changing social mores or failed dreams in American society.

He based his early Americans on himself. When he needed a few more models he did not look far. His cousin Minny Temple gave him the basis for Daisy, for Isabel, and for Milly. Oliver Wendell Holmes and John Gray helped for other characters. His friends from Boston whom he befriended again in Italy and who also appear in these letters, Francis Boott and his daughter Lizzie, gave him Osmond and Pansy and Adam and Maggie. He needed only a few Americans and himself to feed his rich imagination. And he needed a couple of ideas, the sort of ideas that William's friends in his metaphysical club would not have much interest in. These came to him easily and simply. He formulated them, on the basis of his feelings and his observations, in a letter to William written from Malvern in 1870, attacking English women.

> I revolt from their dreary deathly want of—what shall I call it?—Clover Hooper has it—intellectual grace—Minny Temple has it—moral spontaneity. They live wholly in the realm of the cut & dried. . . . I find myself reflecting with peculiar complacency on American women. When I think of their frequent beauty & grace & elegance & alertness,

their cleverness & self-assistance (if it be simply in the matter of toilet) & compare them with English girls, living up to their necks among comforts & influences & advantages wh. have no place with us, my bosom swells with affection & pride. (2: 314–15)

The name of his cousin Minny Temple, who was two years younger than James, appears regularly in these letters. In the summer of 1865, after the Civil War, she tried to locate a room for James and Oliver Wendell Holmes Junior, who would become one of her admirers, in North Conway where she was staying, only to find that there was only one bed in the room. James and Holmes would have to share, which caused James to write to Holmes: "If you don't mind it, *I* don't, as the young lady said when the puppy dog licked her face" (1: 124).

As James began to travel in Europe in 1869, Minny, who was slowly dying of tuberculosis, was still hoping to visit Italy; she had come close to asking him to take her there. But he was traveling alone. From Brescia in September 1869 he asked in a P.S.: "What of M. Temple's coming to Italy?" (2: 99), and again he asked the same question a week later from Venice. Once more the following February from Malvern he wrote: "A[unt] Kate mentions that Mrs. Post [a cousin] has asked Minny to go abroad with her. Is it even so?" (293). And then later that month in a letter to Alice he said: "I have been very sorry to hear of Minny's fresh hemmorhages [*sic*]—& feel glad to have lately written her a long letter" (309). When his father wrote in March 1870 to tell him, still in Malvern, that Minny was very ill, he replied: "I was of course deeply interested in your news about poor Minny. It is a wondrous thing to think of the possible extinction of that immense little spirit. . . . But something tells me that there is something too much of Minny to disappear for some time yet—more life than she has yet lived out" (323).

Minny died on 8 March 1870 when James was still at Malvern. When he heard the news he wrote two letters, one to his mother and one to his brother William. These letters, which are in the Houghton Library where many James family papers are housed, are among his most remarkable and ambiguous. Odd and confused in tone, they remain open to many interpretations. A note at the bottom of the first of them as it appears in these volumes states: "The original ms. is now damaged. The bracketed, italicized insertions are taken from an examination of *HJL* 1 [Leon Edel's edition]. It is possible that Edel saw the undamaged manuscripts" (2: 340). A note at the end of the second uses a small variation: "It is possible that Edel worked from an undamaged manuscript" (348).

These two letters have become even more interesting because of the sharp and fascinating commentary on them by Lyndall Gordon, whose book is, as I have said elsewhere, the best single book that has been written about James. Gordon considered, for example, James's mother's letter breaking the news, with regrets for "dear bright little Minny" (123). Gordon wrote about James's reply: "James grovelled over this morsel of praise: 'God bless you dear Mother for the words. What a pregnant reference in future years.' This young man, who had savaged Dickens and Whitman, could contemplate his mother's banality as a marvel of insight—a measure of her power over him at the age of twenty-seven." Gordon also considered those brief questions about Minny that James had asked in his letters from Brescia and from Venice. "There was a wilful blindness in the way he would not grasp the gravity of her illness and the urgency of her pleas to him to take her on" (104).

After Minny's death, James, Gordon wrote, "tried to impress on his conscience the fact of loss, but what he actually felt was all gain. . . . He told William: 'While I sit spinning my sentences she is *dead*'" (124). In some way her death and his act of writing were linked, as though her vitality had passed to him. Gordon is interested in James as an artist mourning his cousin in the short time after her death and then suddenly working out ways in which he would make use of her life in the future. In Gordon's version of this story, which is carefully argued and not easy to summarize, James felt "enlarged" by Minny's death (124): "She was to fill, not empty, his life" (125).

James's way of handling his mother, however, praising her banality "as a marvel of insight," was not only a sign of her power over him, but also of his over her. His tone was a necessary refusal to take her seriously, a way of keeping her at a distance. It is what many young men do with their mothers. Also, James at twenty-seven had never experienced the death of anyone he knew well before. ("I have been hearing all my life of the sense of loss wh. death leaves behind it:—now for the first time I have a chance to learn what it amounts to," he wrote [*CL* 2: 343].) While he could read several languages and make many fine distinctions, he was, from an emotional point of view, unusually inexperienced. This mixture of pure intelligence about books and places and real obtuseness about difficult emotions was, as it remains, quite a common condition for a young man of his type.

He was also three thousand miles away, unable to express his responses to his cousin's death in normal conversations over days with others who had known her. ("I wish I were at home to hear & talk about her," he wrote [337].) Instead, he had to put his thoughts down on paper. No one should be surprised that these were confused and that, as he tried to let the fact of her death soak in, his tone suggested many contradictory feelings. James sought to console himself with the thought that some good might come of her death, that she might live fruitfully in the memory of those who had known her, or that she had been destined not to live and would not have been happy in full healthy adulthood.

Nonetheless, there is something odd in opening the letter to his mother on the death of Minny by saying that he had "been spending the morning letting the awakened swarm of old reccollections [sic] and associations flow into my mind—almost *enjoying* the exquisite pain they provoke" (336). He moved in the letter from pure sorrow and regret to attempting to say more complicated things. Referring to the fact, for example, that Minny had no personal fortune and could not have thrived in the confines of the domestic sphere, he wrote: "No one who ever knew her can have failed to look at her future as a sadly insoluble problem—& we almost all had imagination enough to say, to ourselves, at least, that life—poor narrow life—contained no place for her" (2: 338). He ended his letter: "My letter doesn't read over-wise; but I have written off my unreason" (339).

It was clear, in his letter to William, however, that he had a good deal more unreason to get out of his system. "A few short hours have amply sufficed to more than reconcile me to the event & to make it seem the most natural," he wrote,

> the happiest, fact, almost in her whole career. So it seems, at least, on reflection: to the eye of feeling there is something immensely moving in the sudden & complete extinction of a vitality so exquisite & so apparently infinite as Minny's. But what most occupies me, as it

will have done all of you at home, is the thought of how her whole life seemed to tend & hasten, visibly audibly, sensibly, to this consummation. Her character may be almost literally said to have been without practical application to life. She seems a sort of experiment of nature—an attempt, a specimen or example—a mere subject without an object. She was at any rate the helpless victim & toy of her own intelligence—so that there is positive relief in thinking of her being removed from her own heroic treatment & placed in kinder hands. (341–42)

It is hard at this point not to wish that someone from Porlock had arrived in Malvern to distract James as he wrote, or that someone at the Houghton Library had further damaged the manuscript of this letter before Edel got his hands on it. Because it gets worse:

Among the sad reflections that her death provokes, for me, there is none sadder than this view of the gradual change & reversal of our relations: I slowly crawling from weakness & inaction & suffering into strength & health & hope: she sinking out of brightness & youth into decline & death. It's almost as if she had passed away—as far as I am concerned—from having served her purpose that of—standing well within the world, inciting & inviting me onward by all the bright intensity of her example. (342–43)

James, like most artists, knew what he was doing only some of the time. He did not realize at the time of Minny's death that he would devote his life to the writing of fiction, although he might have guessed. He did not coldly and ruthlessly set out to use his cousin. His plans for his work were mostly tentative. Minny made her way into his fiction gradually and then forcefully, precisely because her life and her death haunted him in complex ways. He saw what he could make her become. "Greatness in a novelist," Gordon observed, "is a power to see people not only as they are but as they might be" (142). In the creation of Isabel Archer, James freed Minny from death, from economic constraints, but, most important, as Gordon points out, he freed her imagination.

Her memory, in turn, freed James's imagination. It is a part of his mixture of deep self-absorption and steely and manipulative determination, much of which is evident in these letters, that he took what she gave him without any hesitation. In his travels, as in his childhood, he had learned something besides Boston decorum. In 1880 when the serialization of *The Portrait of a Lady* began, he received a letter from Boston, from Grace Norton, saying that the story interested her but suggesting that James had based Isabel on his dead cousin. James, in his reply, stood his ground as a novelist in the most magisterial way, using a tone, managing "an energy of statement," that might put Boston back in its place: "In truth everyone, in life, is incomplete, and it is [in] the work of art that in reproducing them one feels the desire to fill them out, to justify them, as it were. I am delighted I interest you; I think I shall to the end" (*HJL* 2: 324).

WORKS BY HENRY JAMES

CL   *The Complete Letters of Henry James, 1855–1872.* Ed. Pierre A. Walker and Greg W. Zacharias. 2 vols. Lincoln: U of Nebraska P, 2006.

CS   *Complete Stories: 1874–1884.* New York: Library of America, 1999.

HJL *Henry James Letters.* Ed. Leon Edel. 4 vols. Cambridge: Belknap P of Harvard UP, 1974–84.

WHJ *William and Henry James: Selected Letters.* Ed. Ignas K. Skrupskelis and Elizabeth M. Berkeley. Charlottesville: U of Virginia P, 1997.

OTHER WORKS CITED

Bosanquet, Theodora. *Henry James at Work.* Ed. Lyall H. Powers. Ann Arbor: U of Michigan P, 2009.

Gordon, Lyndall. *A Private Life of Henry James: Two Women and His Art.* New York: Norton, 1998.

Jobe, Steven H., and Susan Gunther, eds. *Dearly Beloved Friends: Henry James's Letters to Younger Men.* Ann Arbor: U of Michigan P, 2002.

Zorzi, Rosella Mamoli. *Amato ragazzo: Lettere a Hendrik C. Andersen (1899–1915).* Venezia: Marsilio, 2000.

CHAPTER TEN

All a Novelist Needs

The first entries in Henry James's notebooks that offer us a shadow of Adam Verver in *The Golden Bowl* appeared on 22 May 1892. James had been reading an article in the *Revue des Deux Mondes* on "La Vie Americaine." He began to think of somebody "civilized, large, rich, complete, but strongly characterised, but essentially a *product*. Get the action—the action in which to launch him—it should be a big one. I have no difficulty in *seeing* the figure—it *comes*, as I look at it" (*CN* 70).

Five years earlier, in another notebook entry, James set down the first vague shadow of what would become the "action in which to launch him" (32–33). It arose from something that his sister Alice had mentioned to him—the story that a widower's daughter was opposing her father's remarriage (32–33). This became the precise seed for the story "The Marriages," published in 1891. The protagonist of "The Marriages" was Adela Chart, whose father was about to remarry a woman named Mrs. Churchley. Adela's consternation at the new mother was partly based on the pious memory of her dead mother but also arose from something powerful that pervades the story: Adela's closeness to her father and her sexual jealousy of the woman who had won her father's affections. The story, when it was published, pleased Robert Louis Stevenson, who wrote to James from Samoa: "From this perturbed and hunted being expect but a line, and that line shall be but a whoop for Adela. O she's delicious, delicious; I could live and die with Adela" (348). Stevenson went on to compose a number of stanzas in praise of Adela Chart. For example: "I pore on you, dote on you, clasp you to heart, / I laud, love, and laugh at you, Adela Chart, / And thank my dear maker the while I admire / That I can be neither your husband nor sire" (350).

James, like many writers before him, including Stevenson, managed to embody in his characters themes and ideas that Sigmund Freud would subsequently formulate. The idea of a widowed father and his only child, a young unmarried daughter, dramatized in a shifting set of scenes, each with an aura of something unsettlingly sexual, would have intrigued James once it occurred to him. It did occur to him for "The Marriages" and once again on 28 November 1892 when he wrote in his notebook of "a simultaneous marriage, in Paris, (or only 'engagement' as yet, I believe) of a father and a daughter—an only daughter. The daughter—American of course—is engaged to a young Englishman, and the father, a widower and still youngish, has sought in marriage at exactly the same time an American girl of very much the same age as his daughter" (*CN* 74).

In the scenario that James set out, the father did not lose his daughter because of the two new arrivals into their family; rather, they were thrown together a great deal more. This was because the daughter's husband and the father's wife already had known each other; the young husband "would have married [the father's new wife] if she had had any money. She was poor—the father was very rich, and *that* was her inducement to marry the father" (74). Thus as the father and daughter spent time together, so too did the new husband and the young wife. "The whole situation," James wrote, "works in a kind of inevitable rotary way—in what would be called a vicious circle" (74). James went on to note that "[a] necessary basis for all this must have been an intense and exceptional degree of attachment between the father and daughter—he peculiarly paternal, she passionately filial" (75). He saw the story as "a short tale" and a son-in-law who is French and poor "but has some high social position or name" and is "clever, various, inconstant, amiable, cynical, unscrupulous" (75). His other three characters, James thought, would be "all intensely American."

Three years later, as James took stock of the ideas for new books that were in his head, he listed six possibilities, two of which he did not write, but four of which became novels. One, "La Mourante," was to deal with "the girl who is dying, the young man and the girl he is engaged to" (146); this became *The Wings of the Dove* (1902). Another he called in his notes "The Promise," and this became *The Other House* (1896). Another novel he listed by its actual subsequent title *The Awkward Age* (1899). And one more he named as "The Marriages," adding in parentheses: "what a pity

I've used that name!" (146). He summarized the plot: "the Father and Daughter, with the husband of the one and the wife of the other entangled in a mutual passion, an intrigue" (146). This became *The Golden Bowl* (1904).

For the reader, there is, with James, often a real fascination in attempting to find an autobiographical base for his best fiction or in exploring why certain themes and topics continued to interest him. Nonetheless, to find characters from his life and suggest that he based the characters in his fiction on them is sometimes to miss the point of what he was really doing. As James imagined his books, he saw life as shadow and the art he produced as substance. He believed that language and form, the tapestry of the novel, could produce something much richer and more substantial than mere life, could produce something that offered what was chaotic and fascinating, a sort of complex and golden completion.

It is often as useful to look at a drama already in the making as the seed for James's work as much as an individual character. He was interested in, as his initial inspiration, scenes as much as souls. He made his characters out of the dramatic moments he created for them, treating moral conflicts and matters of secrecy, infidelity, and power with infinite subtlety. In his work a single look, a single moment of recognition, a single ambiguous resolution took on enormous force, became the fuel that powers the great engine of his novels. He dramatized the intensity in the relations between people, playing freedom against pattern, restriction against openness, and dark chaos against harmony.

In the preface to *The Golden Bowl*, written for the New York Edition in 1909, James apologized for the "fewness" of the characters in the book, "the fact that my large demand is made for a group of agents who may be counted on the fingers of one hand. . . . but the scheme of the book, to make up for that, is that we shall really see about as much of them as a coherent literary form permits" (*FW* 1325).

James's friends Francis and Lizzie Boott and their relationship were infused with James's art, as Lyndall Gordon has put it. They are essential creatures for anyone considering the roots of two of James's best novels. In a letter to Lizzie in 1874, after a visit to her father's apartment, James wrote how pleasant it might be "to live in that grave, picturesque old house"

(164). He added: "I have a vague foreboding that I shall, some day." In *Portrait*, Gilbert Osmond and his daughter would not, Edel writes, actually "resemble Frank and Lizzie Boott; but the image of the villa, and of the couple in it, was to serve [James's] need in the novel that was slowly taking shape in his consciousness" (296). Edel goes on: "Perhaps we may discern also . . . the germ of a much later subject . . . for in the observed relationship of a father and a daughter leading a self-sufficient life, he had the theme of an ultimate novel as well" (296). Five years after the publication of *The Portrait of a Lady*, a shift in the Bootts' relationship helped lead James to the plot of *The Golden Bowl*, although he would not begin the book for another seventeen years. In 1886, Lizzie Boott, still living in Florence with her father, married the painter Frank Duveneck. Soon after the wedding, James wrote to Lizzie's father, introducing his close friend Constance Fenimore Woolson, who was coming to Florence, asking Francis Boott to look after her there. As Gordon has written about this introduction, James "had no wish to promote a marriage between Boott and Miss Woolson; his interest lay in their capacities to generate an alternative world which could house his imagination" (204). In other words, James in London could contemplate the four of them in Florence—the father severed from his only daughter, to whom he was devoted, by her marriage, and the arrival of the outsider to offer comfort or provide company for the father. All four living in close proximity.

This is all a novelist needs, nothing exact or precise, no character to be based on an actual person, but a configuration, something distant that can be mulled over, guessed at, dreamed about, imagined, a set of shadowy relations that the writer can begin to put substance on. Changing details, adding shape, but using always something, often from years back, that had captured the imagination, or mattered somehow to the hidden self, however fleetingly or mysteriously.

James was not a moralist, although he had a special interest in morality as a kind of poetics. He relished what right and wrong looked like and sounded like; he became a connoisseur of these concepts for their shape, their aura. And of course he loved what he could do with them. Someone who, in another novelist's hands, could be presented as a villain was, once captured by James's all-embracing and all-forgiving and oddly ironic gaze, a trapped heroine until terms such as "villain" and "heroine" melted into meaninglessness.

This offers us a clue about James's late style. By the time he began to write *The Golden Bowl* in Lamb House in Rye in 1903 his imagination was at its most delicate and refined. His interest in the mechanics of the novel was also at its most ironic and pure. He saw the immense dramatic possibilities in withholding what was expected in a novel about treachery and discovery, innocence and experience. He saw a new shape for the novel in which, as Gordon has written, "manners were merely a starting point, the outermost rind of hidden lives. The deep structure of the great works was still, as always, allegory: evil, renunciation, and the salvation of the soul" (337). Yet even these terms, despite their correctness here, are too large and vague because James sought to offer them, in a tone of full and sweet understanding, to a single and frail human consciousness. Maggie Verver in *The Golden Bowl* stands only for herself. The flickering of her conscious will and her unconscious soul and the subtlety of her responses cannot be summarized nor easily rendered. She is made with many tones, using many patterns. Thoughts and things thus come to her in all their complexity; she deals with them accordingly. For this dramatizing of her consciousness, and of the action that takes place around her, we need a language of infinite suggestion and layered nuance.

This language enacts levels of feeling and knowing in ways that are both precise and indirect, both forensic and poetic. The late style of James suggests that feeling and knowing are open-ended and can lead, even in the bleakest circumstances, to something like forgiveness, the glossing over of unpure motives, the creation of harmony based on language as a beautiful and ambiguous way of healing pain. James came to this style gradually and by necessity, not because he needed a language that was more playful and vague, but because he needed, despite all his qualms, and in a way that mattered to him, a tone that was morally serious, that would measure up to and mediate between the yearning of his characters for completion and the limits that life, despite all its intense variety, offered to them. *The Golden Bowl*, James's last important work of fiction, finds his talent as a stylist and as a novelist at its most supreme.

WORKS BY HENRY JAMES

CN   *The Complete Notebooks of Henry James*. Ed. Leon Edel and Lyall H. Powers. New York: Oxford UP, 1987.

FW   *French Writers; Other European Writers; the Prefaces to the New York Edition*. Ed. Leon Edel and Mark Wilson. New York: Library of America, 1984. Vol. 2 of *Literary Criticism*.

OTHER WORKS CITED

Edel, Leon. *Henry James: The Conquest of London*. New York: Lippincott, 1953.

Gordon, Lyndall. *A Private Life of Henry James: Two Women and His Art*. New York: Norton, 1998.

Stevenson, Robert Louis. *The Biographical Edition of the Works of Robert Louis Stevenson*. New York: Scribners, 1912.

CHAPTER ELEVEN

The Later Jameses

Review of Susan E. Gunter. *Alice in Jamesland: The Story of Alice Howe Gibbens James*. Lincoln: U of Nebraska P, 2009.

Review of Paul Fisher. *House of Wits: An Intimate Portrait of the James Family*. New York: Holt, 2008.

At the end of R. W. B. Lewis's *The Jameses: A Family Narrative* there is an appendix, entitled "The Later Jameses" (595–641), which is a godsend for novelists, geneticists, and anthropologists, to name just three groups who might take an interest in what happened to the James family between the death of Henry in 1916 and 1991, the year the book was published. Readers of Susan E. Gunter's *Alice in Jamesland*, a fascinating new biography of the formidable wife of William James, which ends in 1922 with her death, will be eager to know, for example, what happened to Alice's youngest son Aleck, born in 1890, of whom Gunter paints a tender portrait. Of all of the family, he seemed the most vulnerable and the most sweetly indifferent to the legacy of the name he had inherited. Despite his father's strict views, Aleck appears as a free spirit.

In Lewis's book we discover that Aleck became a painter, which was what he wanted to be: that he remained happily married to the woman of his choice, despite his mother's early views on her, and that, while his brother Harry made money and the next brother Billy married money, Aleck devoted his life to his art. Knowing about him is like knowing about the fate of the characters in *Middlemarch*. Slowly, with these books, the life of each member of the James family is being charted and, by implication, the history of many human types, as they circle each other, nourish each other, and damage each other, is being written.

Alice in Jamesland matches Jean Strouse's masterly biography of the other Alice James, William and Henry's sister, the one who stayed in bed, and Jane Maher's *Biography of Broken Fortune*, the story of the two younger siblings, Wilkie and Bob, who fought in the American Civil War. Gunter offers an ingeniously plotted micro-history of the period and its domestic life and throws light on the personalities of two American geniuses. So, also, *House of Wits: An Intimate Portrait of the James Family* adds to and enriches what we already know from R. W. B. Lewis's history of the family, from Albert Habegger's *The Father*, a life of Henry James Senior, and from the several biographies of William James and Henry James the novelist, including Leon Edel's five-volume biography. Slowly, the Jameses are matching the Bonapartes and the Kennedys. Every scrap of paper they left unburned is being studied for its significance.

Toward the end of his book (459), R. W. B. Lewis notes the continued presence of Jameses in Bailieborough in County Cavan, Ireland, until the death of Bobby James there in 1932 at the age of ninety-two. It was from Bailieborough sometime between 1789 and 1794 that William James, later of Albany, set out for the United States. In his will the elder James attempted effectively to disinherit Henry, the fifth of his thirteen children, because of his drinking habits. His inheritance restored, Henry James Senior devoted his life to free thinking, replacing his father's stern authority with his own immense questing spirit. In 1840, he married Mary Walsh, also of Irish Presbyterian stock, whom he had met at her family home in Washington Square in New York.

They had two children in quick succession. William was born in 1841. Eighteen months later, Henry James Senior, who had a tendency toward restlessness, wrote to Emerson, whose work he admired and whom he had befriended, that "[a]nother fine little boy . . . preaches to me that I must be settled at home" (qtd. in Fisher 71). This was Henry, who became the novelist.

But the father had no intention of settling at home, much to Emerson's horror. "Every week," Emerson wrote, "I hear of some conspicuous American who is embarking for France or Germany and every such departure is a virtual postponement of the traveller's own work & endeavour" (72).

In England, James, who had crossed the ocean with his wife, his sister-in-law, and two infant sons, befriended Carlyle, who wrote to Emerson: "James is a very good fellow, better and better as we see him more—

Something shy and skittish in the man; but a brave heart intrinsically. ... He confirms an observation of mine ... that a stammering man is never a worthless one" (77). Jane Carlyle noticed James's wooden leg, a result of an accident when he was thirteen. He was, she wrote, "'[N]ot a bad man ... nor altogether a fool'—but he has only one leg—that is to say only one real available leg—the other ... consisting entirely of cork— Now a man needs to take certain precautions ... to use some sort of *stick* instead of trusting to Providence as this Mr James does. So that every time he moves in the room ... one awaits with horror to see him rush down amongst the tea-cups, or walk out thro the window glass, or pitch himself foremost into the grate!" His wife and sister-in-law, she noted, "giggled incessantly, and wore *black* stockings with light-colour[e]d dresses."

The James menage moved from London to Paris and then back to England where they rented Frogmore Cottage at Windsor from the Duchess of Kent. It was here Henry Senior suffered an attack of hysteria, which filled him with fear, as, alone in the house, he sensed "some damned shape squatting invisible to [him] within the precincts of the room" (81). This hallucination, Fisher points out, could easily have been caused by drink, but its shivering victim later came to the view that he had undergone what Swedenborg called "vastation." Thus the Swedish philosopher replaced Emerson and Carlyle in Henry James Senior's pantheon of saviors.

Once back in Manhattan and then in Albany where he moved for two years, the victim of the vastation began to correspond with other Swedenborgians, calling his next son, born in 1845, Garth Wilkinson after one of the most enthusiastic of these. Another son, Bob, was born in 1846. The Jameses finally moved back to Manhattan and into a house, their first, at West Fourteenth Street. Their last child Alice was born in 1848.

The father of the five young Jameses did not cease his explorations: he flirted with socialism and with free love; he wrote many letters and gave lectures to whomever would listen. His wife, as Fisher makes clear, "learned to manage [his] health and emotional stability" (106) and to ignore his more recondite and peculiar views. Of erotic passion, he wrote to a friend: "Who will ever be caught in that foolish snare again? I did nothing but tumble into it from my boyhood to my marriage; since which great disillusioning—yes!—I feel that the only lovable person is the one who does not permit himself to be loved" (106–7). His wife, despite these views of his, which were often expressed loudly and widely, coped with him sweetly, deftly, with an apparent innocence about what she was doing, as Fisher writes. "Under Mary's influence, Henry tempered passionate unconventionality with Victorian restraint—a paradox he would bequeath to his children" (107).

It is fascinating to study the creation of two of these children—the writers William and Henry James—to watch how much of their ambition and achievement came into being precisely because of the attention their parents brought to bear on them, or how much came into being despite that very energy, or in ways which seemed to evade or oppose its force. As you read Gunter and Fisher, it is hard not to wonder if these artists became who they were by some sort of design, from the education they received and from a set of circumstances put in place very early in their lives.

In the second half of the nineteenth century we can watch other sets of siblings also become artists. W. B. Yeats and his brother Jack, the painter, for example; Heinrich and Thomas Mann; Virginia Woolf and Vanessa Bell. In the case of all four families, there was a dynamic at work that involved a struggle for power, or something like power, between siblings, a sort of fierce ambition within families for recognition and escape. In the case of all four families—the Yeatses, the Manns, the Stephenses, the Jameses—the parents seemed to shine a light on some of their children and to leave the others to their own devices. In these families where geniuses were nurtured, there were also damaged ones begging for attention. Just as the artists lived in the light, their siblings lurked in the shadows: Lily and Lolly Yeats, for example, who ran the Cuala Press, one of them as clever and talented as her brothers, the other difficult and cantankerous, both uneasy and unfulfilled; or the two Mann sisters who both committed suicide; or the brothers, step-brothers and step-sister of Virginia Woolf and Vanessa Bell who seemed to orbit the two artists like lesser planets. Or Wilkie, Bob, and Alice James. In any study of these families, the work and theories of Foucault about power and control, rather than those of Freud, seem to best explain how things were managed and what the results were.

The formal education of William and Henry James involved what the latter would call "small vague spasms of school" (Fisher 115) with many changes and tutors. But in the foreground was their father, at home all the time, filled with ideas and ambitions, never silent. It is perhaps too easy to say for sure that the sense of steely finish and the rigorous edge in the works of William and Henry James arose from their father's precise lack of these, that the best education they got was from watching him and deciding not to be like him. What the Jameses got from their mother, which remains more difficult to describe, may have been equally influential.

The move back to Europe in 1855 also had the effect of taking the two intelligent teenagers, so different from each other, away from any peer group or place that might limit them or give them complacent roots. The family went to London first, then Paris, then Geneva, then London again, then Paris once more, then Boulogne-sur-Mer. They returned to America in 1858 to live at Newport, Rhode Island, but the following year the entire family plus Aunt Kate (their mother's sister) returned once more to Geneva. As they moved, Henry Senior seemed to grow increasingly restless. "Alice would remember," Fisher writes, "that Henry [senior] abandoned his family, every so often, for a few days at a time. In fact, certain Continental cities would be perpetually marked with the memory of his mercurial departures and his 'sudden returns.' Quixotically, fresh from some train or steamer, Henry could reappear 'at the end of 36 hours, having left to be gone a fortnight'" (148–49).

In 1860, the James family returned to America again, and to Newport. William took classes in painting, and Henry followed suit, but in a half-hearted way. As talk of civil war began, it was unclear what either of them, so out of touch with America, would do.

Their father, in the meantime, on the advice of Emerson, enrolled his two younger sons—whom he and his wife viewed as less talented, almost less worthy, than their two older siblings—in an academy, run by an abolitionist agitator Frank Sanborn, where Hawthorne's son Julian and John Brown's daughter were also pupils. Thoreau guided the students in walks in the woods.

In April 1861, at the time of Lincoln's call to arms, William and Henry James were, at nineteen and eighteen, the exact age when young men were joining the Union army. Many of their friends and a few of their cousins were enlisting. William, instead, went to Harvard. Henry may or may not have had his famous accident while fighting a fire two days after the call to arms. Fisher allows for the possibility, but it seems rather unlikely. This "horrid even if an obscure hurt" (Fisher 177), as Henry James later coyly called it, meant that he could not join the army. Instead, in 1862, with his father's approval, his younger sibling Wilkie enlisted, and in 1863 brother Bob followed him.

Both Wilkie and Bob, still teenagers, witnessed the most appalling carnage. Wilkie was badly injured. Bob was deeply shaken by what he saw. Neither of them ever fully recovered from the war. Neither

> would find the challenges of ordinary life as stimulating as the dramatic, draining, and emotionally fraught experiences of war. After the close bonds of soldiering and the heightened adrenaline of battle, these young men would find it difficult to return to lives where they were no longer heroes, where they in fact felt somewhat second class. (Fisher 186)

In the meantime, Alice James, the youngest of the five, was also damaged by being what was jokingly called a native of the James family. Alice was intelligent, witty, sharp, and, within a limited circle in which she felt relaxed, almost brilliant. But she was also sensitive, awkward, self-conscious, and fragile. "One feels," Leon Edel says, "that she doffed her swaddling-clothes but to don a spiritual straitjacket" (qtd. in Strouse 82). "She was," Jean Strouse writes,

> growing up into a world in which she still seemed to have no place, and her spirit rebelled against the enforced uselessness of a female adolescence that coincided with the greatest national crisis of the century. Since her nature *was* ardent, she had to struggle constantly to quench its unruly assertions. It was the struggle of a lifetime. (82)

It is clear that Mary James applied herself to the welfare of her talented and sensitive second son. In Henry's tender writings about his mother, especially after her death, and in the surviving letters between them, one notes Mary James's intelligence, kindness, and maternal indulgence. It is less easy to see what the mother did for Alice, other than force her into a routine of dullness and duty. Such pressure may have been customary for young women of the age but was not helpful for someone whose background and upbringing were as unsettled and unusual as Alice and whose personality was as brittle.

In 1864, the Jameses moved to Boston. William traveled and studied medicine; Henry began to publish short stories. In 1869 Henry left for England, then began to travel on the European mainland. Although he would return home in 1870, the scene was set for his long exile. Fisher is enlightening about the financial cost of this expatriatism. While the new family home in Quincy Street had cost twenty thousand dollars and while Wilkie and Bob had been sent to work, both eventually being employed as payroll clerks for a railroad company in the Midwest, Henry James's first year in Europe cost his family two thousand dollars.

In 1872, William James began to teach physiology at Harvard, thus beginning a long association with the university. Henry, who had published his first novel and was writing many pieces for magazines, returned to Europe, this time to Rome, then Paris and finally in 1876 settling in London. When he was visited in Italy by William, who suggested that he should marry, "[h]e refused point-blank," as William reported to Bob (Fisher 306). Both Wilkie and Bob, on the other hand, soon married rich women, Bob's fiancée arriving at the James home in Boston wearing "two thousand dollars on her fingers . . . and five thousand dollars hung 'pendant from her ears,'" much to the horror of the family, who disliked display and vulgarity (310).

Since Henry had escaped to Europe and Alice spent her time in bed or recovering from sessions there and Wilkie and Bob had moved away (or been banished) and found wives, the attention of Henry Senior and his wife, who longed to give advice and to interfere in their children's lives, was now focused sharply on William. In his early thirties, he was still living at home under their watchful eye (317). Like Henry his brother and Alice his sister, William was much given to illnesses that could not be fully explained. He was often miserable. Early in 1876, his father arrived home one evening to announce, perhaps playfully, that he had caught a glimpse of the woman who was to be William's wife. Her name was Alice Howe Gibbens. Although "more intellectually engaged than Mary James," Fisher writes, "she reminded Henry Senior very much of his wife:

she rated as the same kind of no-nonsense marriage prospect that Mary Walsh had been almost forty years before. Hence Henry's view that she was just what his son needed" (321).

Alice in Jamesland gives a sharp, subtle, and sympathetic portrait of the woman whom Henry James Senior announced would be suitable for his ambitious and neurotic son. The fact that Alice Gibbens emerges as the most sane member of the James family does not perhaps mean much. Luckily for us all, the family did not value sanity as highly as, say, talent, or the molding of talent towards genius. In her biography, Gunter manages to re-create, with tact and care, the life of a wife and mother in an upper-middle-class Boston household during this period. She charts what it was like to look after one of the most needy and talented figures to emerge from that class. She shows how, despite much self-sacrifice and self-suppression, Alice Gibbens actually survived, almost thrived, in this role. Perhaps because she does not dwell as much as she might on the response of Alice James, William's sister, to the new Alice in the family, or does not emphasize the new Alice's general bossiness around other women—most notably Katherine Loring, her sister-in-law Alice's companion, or Theodora Bosanquet, the secretary of her brother-in-law Henry James—or her disapproval of Edith Wharton, she depicts Alice Howe Gibbens James as an admirable figure, filled with strength and understanding, calmly intelligent and immensely capable.

Just as Aunt Kate had burned letters and papers after the death of Henry James Senior and Henry James had lit a number of significant bonfires at Rye towards the end of his life, both Alice Gibbens James and her son Harry burned many letters. Harry destroyed, in fact, all but two bundles of his mother's correspondence, as they did not seem to him to "possess the special interest that attaches more or less to all of my father's letters" (Gunter 318). This makes Susan Gunter's achievement in not only piecing together a life of Alice James but creating a full portrait of her without recourse to guesswork or speculation all the more remarkable.

Perhaps the single event in Alice Gibben's life that caused her determination to create emotional stability around her was her father's suicide in 1865 when she was sixteen. She had survived, Fisher writes, "by becoming a provider, a caretaker, a manager, a pillar" (321). She took responsibility for her two younger sisters and her mother and had, by the time Henry

James Senior laid eyes on her, been teaching for some years at a school for girls in Beacon Hill. Her relationship with William James began slowly and was often filled with uncertainty, mainly due to William's indecision and his highly developed sense of an interior darkness. He was given to being tortured and distraught. "I renounce you," he wrote when they had known each other for more than a year. "Let the eternal tides bear you where they will. In the end they'll bear you round to where I wait for you. I'll feed on death now, but I'll buy the right to eternal life by it" (Fisher 349). But he did not really renounce Alice Gibbens, nor indeed did he feed on death; instead he seemed to enjoy agonizing over the possibility that he might or might not marry her. He was lucky she waited. More than two years after their meeting, they became engaged.

Soon after their marriage, and established in Boston, Alice Gibbens began to work closely with her husband, whose ideas about psychology were slowly developing. When he delivered a series of six lectures entitled "The Brain and the Mind," "the bulk of the outlines," Gunter writes, "and fragments of extant drafts are in Alice's hand" (58). The following year when an article by William appeared in the magazine *Mind* most of the manuscript was also in Alice's hand (60). After their first child was born, he wrote to her: "Dearest, I do feel as if I were related to you by a peculiar kind of tie" (63).

Her independence of mind displayed itself in her attitude to her children. When the doctor instructed that she should not feed her first child between ten at night and six in the morning, she decided to ignore him. "I concluded after much thinking that it was our own affair . . . and so to the great joy of the poor little thing I let him nurse just as often as he chooses" (69). While Gunter emphasizes, with considerable display of evidence, Alice's sexual closeness to William, she also makes clear that Alice's religious beliefs were more traditional and much firmer than William's. When Henry James Senior died, Alice wrote to her husband, who was in England: "If one impression, stronger than all others is left to me from those days, it is the unutterable reality, *realness*, *nearness* of the spiritual world" (71). Alice and William dabbled in spiritualism all of their lives, but Alice seemed to believe in mediums and séances more fervently than William, who was, however, always fascinated by them. They both regularly saw Mrs. Piper, a medium who seemed to know a great deal about them. Alice's involvement increased when she lost her baby son Hermann. Gunter writes with real insight and tenderness about this loss, which haunted Alice James for the rest of her life. Twenty years after it occurred, for example, she wrote to William: "I have such curious dreams, and one unhappy thing keeps recurring. I seem to be wandering in difficult places . . . and always carrying in my arms a baby, whose I know not, a weak ailing child whom I cannot get rid of or lay to rest" (87).

The relationship between Alice James and her brother-in-law Henry, who was visiting Boston when Henry Senior died and his brother William was in England, was close and warm. It must have been a relief for Alice to meet him. His calm reticence, firm ability to listen, and his general equanimity must have come as a surprise. It was not shared by any of his siblings, William included. William, in fact, became jealous of their closeness when he was in England. When he expressed a wish to return, Henry wrote to him: "Your wife strikes me as distinctly *distressed* at the prospect of your return, & she could not restrain her tears as she spoke of it to me today" (74). Alice, in turn, wrote to William about Henry: "My depression last night was not for your postponed return. No dear! it was the after effect of Harry who is to me like a strange perfume, very pleasant but leaving a curious lassitude behind. And he is so good!" William wrote back: "I shiver through & through with longing to be with you & never to leave your side, to melt into your being, to be rolled in your arms & silent in a last embrace" (75).

Alice James was, in fact, besides his own mother, the only American woman with a husband and children whom Henry James came to know well. She made her way into his fiction in three stories written in the early 1880s, when he had been in her company in the aftermath of his father's death, "The Impressions of a Cousin" in which he drew her as steadfast and dutiful, and "Pandora" and "Lady Barbarina" in which he dealt with scenes from her earlier life when, after her father's suicide, the family had lived in Germany. He also used her name, some of her address, and her personality ("a model of stability and love" [257], as Gunter writes) in "The Jolly Corner," one of his last stories, written in 1907. She thus joined his cousin Minny Temple, Lizzie Boott, and his sister Alice. His sister-in-law was clever enough perhaps to allow it to escape her attention that there are elements of her in the formidable figure of Mrs. Newsome in *The Ambassadors*, who did not believe in nonsense. (Alice Gibbens James's view of Rome, for example: "But I belong to the north and not all this beauty can repay me the filth, cruelty and crime-tainted atmosphere of the place" [191]). She must have been helpful as well, since it was her world, as James set about creating *The Bostonians*.

She was also an avid reader of Henry's work, writing to him of his novel *The Tragic Muse*, for example:

> You seem to me to have crossed the border into the kingdom of the Great, into the land where the few, the Masters live and create by laws and immensities of their own. The book is, unlike any other—so new that perhaps people won't take to it today or tomorrow, but its own day is waiting for it. The delightful talk, the serene good nature, the revelation of the artistic nature—it's all wonderfully fine. And it all fits and rests in its own whole. I mean the feeling of structure which it gives me, as does a beautiful piece of architecture. The sensation is rare enough to be reveled in when at last it is vouchsafed. (116–17)

William and Alice built a large house on Irving Street near Harvard and a summer house at Chocorua in New Hampshire. They had four children, Harry, Billy, Peggy, and, finally, a boy whose name changed many times but eventually became Aleck. William in these years was often as restless as his father had been. "No matter where he was," Gunter writes, "someplace else might be better" (127). He traveled alone to Europe and then with his family. He was not an easy traveling companion. During their visit to Europe in 1892, Gunter writes, "the couple fought often during their stay in Florence, usually over children and money. . . . [One] day he came home with paintings, an unauthorized purchase. When she protested, William took a pair of scissors and cut the landscapes into pieces while their son Harry watched in horror" (134).

Henry James, as he observed them, did not envy his brother and sister-in-law their brood or their responsibilities. When William and Alice came to England alone, having left their children in schools on the European mainland, Henry told his friend Francis Boott that if he were in their place, "he would not return to Switzerland to get the children" (140). Four years later he wrote "The Turn of the Screw."

In the end, as Robert Lowell wrote in his poem "Obit," "every hypo-

chondriac is his own prophet." In 1898, at the age of fifty-seven, on a long
and strenuous walk in the Adirondacks, William James damaged his heart.
Alice James was to spend the next twelve years nursing him, traveling
with him to places, especially Bad Nauheim in Germany, in search of a
cure, and worrying in the meantime about her children. Between the ages
of eight and ten, her youngest son Aleck was left with his grandmother
while his parents traveled. Peggy James, who was as sensitive, intelligent,
and vulnerable as her aunt Alice, was placed in unsuitable schools in England while her parents moved uneasily about.

While Gunter charts the difficulties in their marriage, she also emphasizes their closeness and William's gratitude to his wife for her dedication.
"Darling in all seriousness," he wrote to her in 1890 when she had read the
proofs, 1,400 pages, of *The Principles of Psychology*, "you have lifted me
up out of lonely hell. . . . You have redeemed my life from destruction and
crowned me with loving kindness & tender mercy, and my fortunes are
entirely linked with yours" (117). Sixteen years later, he wrote: "Never have
you seemed as near and dear to me as in the past six months. It is a good
thing, little as you think of 'friendship' to have friendship grow deeper
and deeper—after 27 years of matrimony! Isn't it?" (221). The marriage,
as Gunter writes, "was more than either imagined it when they first met:
it was a genuine love story" (221).

Alice's intelligence and her calm involvement in her children's lives
made a considerable difference to her two younger children. While Harry
and Billy, who would eventually marry suitably, had no problems with the
world in which they were brought up—a world of old Boston money and
respectability, matched with a belief in books and ideas—and were careful
not to disappoint their father, Peggy required close attention as she grew
into her teens and suffered a great deal as a young woman. Aleck caused
consternation to his father by his lack of interest in his studies. William
wanted all his sons to go to Harvard. Aleck, who was dyslexic, had no
interest in Harvard. For years he was made miserable, forced to study,
and generally hectored. His mother, at the same time, watched over him
with care, less concerned with his father's ambitions. In the same way, she
watched over Peggy (whose father wrote to the dean of Bryn Mawr that
she was sweet but boring [235]), so that neither of them followed members of the previous generation such as Aunt Alice (who had removed

herself to England, where she suffered still from nervous maladies) or Uncle Bob (who was now drinking heavily and making a total nuisance of himself). This did not prevent Aleck's mother, however, from later trying to stop Aleck's engagement to a young woman of whom she disapproved, although she later grew fond of her.

Henry James took an enormous interest in his three nephews and his niece, growing close to each of them in different ways, much encouraged by their mother. Toward the end of William's life, as Henry's heart also began to show signs of strain, William and Alice crossed the Atlantic to be with Henry in England. Despite his long exile and the many close friendships he had made, it was absolutely clear that Henry had never emotionally left his family and that his sister-in-law, now that he was in distress, was the person he most needed to see. When William went to Bad Neuheim, Alice remained with Henry and then was torn between the two brothers and their illnesses.

Being ill took up all of their waking time. As one got better, the other would get worse. Since they both had suffered from illnesses, many imaginary, all of their lives, as a way of gaining attention or avoiding trouble, neither was quite sure that the other was really sick now. Henry, Gunter writes, "insisted that his brother's condition was a nervous one, just as William insisted that Henry's ailments were the result of melancholia" (266). At one point Alice noted: "William cannot walk and Henry cannot smile" (262). Neither brother wanted to be without her. She wrote to her mother: "Though my presence seems often to be a doubtful blessing I can not be free to go off and risk either of them missing me" (265).

"She was no longer a virtual bride for two brothers," Gunter writes, "she was now literally a life partner to both" (262). It seems unfortunate, to say the least, that Henry's great energy and dedication as a writer were things of the past, because these months as he and his brother fought for the loyalty and attention of Alice Gibbens in London, Rye, Bad Neuheim, and points in between offered a subject to which he could have done great justice—as indeed could have Oscar Wilde.

After William's death in 1910 Alice became active in promoting his work and establishing his reputation. Although Peggy remained close to Henry, and eventually married a friend of his, a man to whom he had once written ardent letters, she noticed on a visit to England the difference between her uncle and her father, essentially the difference between a novelist and a philosopher: "To be quite candid, I miss any of Dad's quality in Uncle Henry—especially any spiritual or speculative turn. Speculative about people yes—but of any abstract occupations of mind I can see no glimmer" (278).

In the last week of his life, William James had asked his wife to promise "that you will see Henry through when he comes to the end" (291). By this time Wilkie and Bob and Alice James were already dead (Wilkie died in 1883, Alice in 1892, Bob in 1910). Henry was the last of the five siblings. He was alone in England as the war broke out. Thus in December 1915 when she received a telegram that he had had a stroke, Alice Gibbens set out for England. Henry was in bed when she arrived, his amanuensis Theodora Bosanquet managing his affairs and often taking dictation from him in his room, where he had delusions, as he lay stricken, that he was Napoleon.

Gunter is gentle about what happened next:

> one of her first tasks was to take authority for Henry's various affairs, a task that, in addition to household management, included negotiating Theodora's involvement. Alice judged that Theodora had done admirably, but the woman looked weary. Slowly but surely, Alice weaned Henry's amanuensis from his side, confident that she was doing what was best for the ailing giant. The doctor advised keeping all visitors away, as they would tire his patient, but Alice feared that Theodora would try to countermand this order, especially in the case of Edith Wharton. When she let a message to Wharton through, Alice reacted quickly and virtually banned the woman from Henry's Chelsea flat. . . . she wanted to give Theodora some sort of settlement if Henry had not remembered her in his will. Theodora represented everything Alice disliked about the women's movement. Alice's vocation had been different: her work, since she resigned her teaching post in 1878, had been unpaid but demanding. She was on firm footing now, doing the work she had done all her life, tasks that she believed were her rightful purview. (293–94)

While Miss Bosanquet might have represented all that Mrs. William James disliked about the women's movement, Edith Wharton must have evoked stronger, more Bostonian, emotions. Once again, Henry James could have written beautifully about his sister-in-law's banishment of both.

Miss Bosanquet later told Leon Edel:

> Edith Wharton ... was such a well-established and firm friend of Henry James, and so very unhappy about his condition. . . . Looking back on those difficult days, I rather imagine that Mrs. James very much preferred having her dau. [Peggy] at hand rather than a secretarial assistant for whom there was so little work. . . . I can only regret more than ever that Mrs. William James appeared to have no use for me or my services after a short time. (294)

As James lay dying, his sister-in-law remained with him day and night. Sometimes he confused her with his mother. After his death, he was cremated, and Alice, who was an expert at evading customs, smuggled his ashes back to the United States. She buried his ashes in Cambridge near the remains of his brother William, his sister Alice, his parents, and her son who had died as a baby.

Later, as the family decided to prepare an edition of Henry James's letters, Alice prevented Edith Wharton's involvement. When the book appeared, she took the view that there had been excessive mention of Wharton. Wharton, in turn, disliked the edition and made this clear in a letter to the family. On receipt of this letter, Peggy wrote to her mother that Wharton's letter "was disgusting—deliberately insulting—and cold. I am very sorry that you sent her the book. She is a minx and not in the least a lady" (316–17). As readers of the volume of letters began to note the unusually amorous tone in some of her brother-in-law's missives to younger men, Alice James, steadfast and loyal to the end, wrote to her son: "people are putting a vile interpretation on those silly letters to young men.—Poor dear Uncle Henry" (317).

WORKS CITED

Lewis, R. W. B. *The Jameses: A Family Narrative*. New York: Farrar, 1991.
Strouse, Jean. *Alice James: A Biography*. Boston: Houghton, 1980.

Silence

From the Notebooks of Henry James: An Unwritten Story

34 D.V.G., January 23d, 1894.

Another incident—"subject"—related to me by Lady G. was that of the eminent London clergyman who on the Dover-to-Calais steamer, starting on his wedding tour, picked up on the deck a letter addressed to his wife, while she was below, and finding it to be from an old lover, and very ardent (an engagement—a rupture, a relation, in short), of which he never had been told, took the line of sending her, from Paris, straight back to her parents—without having touched her—on the ground that he had been deceived. He ended, subsequently, by taking her back into his house to live, but *never* lived with her as his wife. There is a drama in the various things, for her, to which that situation—that night in Paris—might have led. Her immediate surrender to some one else, etc. XXXXX (*CN* 85, 86)

Sometimes when the evening had almost ended Lady Gregory would catch someone's eye for a moment and that would be enough to make her remember. At those tables in the great city she knew not ever to talk about herself, or complain about anything such as the heat, or the dullness of the season, or the antics of an actress; she knew not to babble about banalities, or laugh at things which were not very funny. She focused instead with as much force and care as she could on the gentleman beside her and asked him intelligent, clear questions and then listened with attention to the answers. Listening took more work than talking; she made sure that her companion knew, from the sympathy and sharp light in her eyes, how intelligent she was, and how quietly powerful and deep.

She would suffer only when she left the company. In the carriage on the way home she would stare into the dark, knowing what had happened in those years would not come back, that memories were no use, that there was nothing ahead except darkness. And on the bad nights, after evenings when there had been too much gaiety and brightness, she often wondered if there was much difference between her life now and the years stretching to eternity that she would spend in the grave.

Always then she would write out a list and the writing itself would give her satisfaction. Things to live for. Her son Robert would always come first, and then some of her sisters. She smiled at the thought of erasing one or two of them, and maybe one brother, but no more than one. And then Coole Park, the house in Ireland her husband had left her, or at least left their son, and that she could always return to. She thought of the trees she had planted at Coole, she dreamed of going back there now to study the slow sturdy progress of things as the winter gave way to spring. And there were books and paintings and the way light came into a high room as she pulled the shutters back in the morning. She would add these also to the list.

Below the list was blank paper. It would be easy now, she thought, to fill it with another list. A list of grim facts led by a single inescapable thought—that love had eluded her, that love would not come back, that she was alone and she would have to make the best of being alone.

She crumbled the piece of paper in her hand before she stood up and made her way to the bedroom and prepared for the night. She was glad, or almost glad, that there would be no more outings that week, that no London hostess had the need for a dowager from Ireland at her table for the moment. A woman known for her listening skills and her keen intelligence had her uses, she thought, but not every night of the week.

She had liked being married; she had enjoyed being noticed as the young wife of an old man, had liked the effect her quiet gaze could have on friends of her husband's who thought she might be dull because she was not pretty. She had liked letting them know, carefully, tactfully, keeping her voice low, that she was someone on whom nothing was lost. She had read all the latest books and she chose her words slowly when she came to discuss them. She did not want to seem clever; this was not the effect she sought to have. She made sure that she was silent without seeming shy, polite and reserved without being intimidated. She had no natural grace and she made up for this by having no empty opinions. She took the view that it was a mistake for a woman with her looks ever to show her teeth. In any case, she disliked laughter and preferred to smile using her eyes, softening her gaze in amusement and sympathy.

She disliked her husband only when he came to her at night in those first months; his fumbling and panting, his eager hands and his sour breath gave her a sense which almost amused her that daylight and many layers of clothing and servants and large furnished rooms and chatter about politics or paintings were ways to distract people from feeling a deep revulsion towards each other.

There were times when she saw him in the distance or had occasion to glance at his face in repose when she viewed him as someone who had merely on a whim or a sudden need rescued her or captured her. He was too old to know her, he had seen too much and lived too long to allow anything new, such as a wife thirty-five years his junior, to enter his orbit. In the night, in those early months, as she tried to move towards him to embrace him fully, to offer herself to his dried-up spirit, she found that he was happier fondling obsessively certain parts of her body in the dark as though he were trying to find something he had mislaid. And thus as she attempted to please him, she also tried to make sure that, when he was finished, she would be able gently to turn away from him and face the dark alone as he slept and snored. She longed to wake in the morning and not have to look at his face too closely, his half-opened mouth, his stubbled chin, his grey whiskers, his wrinkled skin.

All over London, she thought, in the hours after midnight in rooms with curtains drawn, silence was broken by grunts and groans and deep sighs. It was lucky, she knew, that it was all done in secret, lucky also that no matter how much they talked of love or faithfulness or the unity of man and wife that no one would ever realize how apart people were in these hours, how deeply and singly themselves, how thoughts came which could never be shared or whispered or made known in any way. This was marriage, she thought, and it was her job to be calm about it. There were times when the grim, dull truth of it almost made her wonder why there was not agitation among right-thinking people to put an end to it once and for all.

Nonetheless, there was in the day almost an excitement about being the wife of Sir William Gregory, of having a role to play in the world. He had been lonely, that much was clear. He had married her because he had been lonely. He longed to travel and he enjoyed the idea now that she would arrange his clothes and distract him and listen to him talk. They could enter dining rooms together as others did, rooms in which an elderly man alone would have appeared out of place, too sad somehow.

And because he knew his way around the world—he had been governor of Ceylon, among other things—he had many old friends and associates, was oddly popular and dependable and cultured and well informed and almost amusing in company. Once they arrived in Cairo therefore, it was natural that they would spend time with the young poet Wilfred Scawen Blunt and his grand wife, that they two couples would dine together and find each other interesting as they discussed poetry lightly and then, as things began to change, argued politics with growing intensity and seriousness.

Wilfred Scawen Blunt. As she lay in the bed with the light out, Lady Gregory smiled at the thought that she would not need ever to write his name down on any list. His name belonged elsewhere; it was a name she might breathe on glass or whisper to herself when things were more grim than she had ever imagined that anything could become. It was a name that might have been etched on her heart if she believed in such things, but she did not.

His fingers were long and beautiful; even his fingernails had a glow of health; his hair was shiny, his teeth white. And his eyes brightened as he spoke; thinking made him smile and when he smiled he exuded a sleek perfection. He was as far from her as a palace was from her house in Coole or as the heavens were from the earth. She liked looking at him as she liked a Bronzino or a Titian and she was careful always to pretend that she also liked looking at his wife, Byron's granddaughter, although she did not.

She thought of them like food, Lady Anne all watery vegetables, or sour, small potatoes, or salted fish, and the poet her husband like lamb cooked slowly for hours with garlic and thyme or goose stuffed at Christmas. And she remembered in her childhood the watchful eye of her mother, her mother making her eat each morsel of bad winter food, leave her plate clean. Thus she forced herself to pay attention to every word Lady Anne said; she gazed at her with soft and sympathetic interest, she spoke to her with warmth and the dull intimacy that one man's wife might have with another, hoping that soon Lady Anne would be calmed and suitably assuaged by this so that she would not notice when Lady Gregory turned her gaze to the poet and ate him up with her eyes.

Blunt was on fire with passion during these evenings, composing letters to the *Times* at the very dining table in support of Ali Bey, arguing in favour of loosening the control which France and England had over Egyptian affairs, cajoling Sir William, who was of course a friend of the editor of the *Times*, to put pressure on the paper to publish his letter and support the cause. Sir William was calm, quiet, watchful, gruff. It was easy for Blunt to feel that he agreed with every point Blunt was making mainly because Blunt did not notice dissent. They arranged for Lady Gregory to visit Ali Bey's wife and family so that she could describe to the English how refined they were and sweet and deserving of support.

The afternoon when she returned was unusually hot. Her husband, she found, was in a deep sleep so that she did not disturb him. When she went in search of Blunt, she was told by the maid that Lady Anne had a severe headache brought on by the heat and would not be appearing for the rest of the day. Her husband the poet could be found in the garden or in the room he kept for work where he often spent the afternoons. Lady Gregory found him in the garden; Blunt was excited to hear about her visit to Bey's family and ready to show her a draft of a poem he had composed that morning on the matter of Egyptian freedom. She went to his study with him, not realizing until she was in the room and the door was closed that the study was in fact an extra bedroom the Blunts had taken, no different from the Gregorys' own room except for a large desk and books and papers strewn on the floor and on the bed.

As Blunt read her the poem, he crossed the room and turned the key in the lock as though it were a normal act, what he always did as he read a new poem. He read it a second time and then left the piece of paper down on the desk and moved towards her and held her. He began to kiss her. Her only thought was that this might be the single chance she would get in her life to associate with beauty. Like a tourist in the vicinity of a great temple, she thought it would be a mistake to pass it by; it would be something she would only regret. She did not think it would last long or mean much. She also was sure that no one had seen them come down this corridor; she presumed that her husband was sleeping; she believed that no one would find them and that she could leave soon and it would never be mentioned again between them.

Later, when she was alone and checking that there were no traces of what she had done on her skin or on her clothes, the idea that she had lain naked with the poet Blunt in a locked room on a hot afternoon and that he had, in a way which was new to her, made her cry out in ecstasy frightened her. She had been married less than two years, time enough to know how deep her husband's pride ran, and how cold he was to those who had crossed him, and how sharp and decisive he could be. They had left their child in England so they could travel to Egypt even though Sir William knew how much it pained her to be separated in this way from Robert. Were Sir William to be told that she had been visiting the poet in his private quarters, she believed he could ensure that she never saw her child again. Or he could live with her in pained silence and barely managed contempt. Or he could send her home. The corridors were full of servants, figures watching. She thought it a miracle that she had managed once to be unnoticed. She believed that she might not be so lucky a second time.

Over the weeks that followed and in London when she returned home, she discovered that Wilfred Scawen Blunt's talents as a poet were minor compared to his skills as an adulterer. Not only could he please her in ways which were daring and astonishing but he could ensure that they would not be discovered. The sanctity of his calling required him to have silence, solitude, and quarters which his wife had no automatic right to enter. Blunt composed his poems in a locked room. He rented this room away from his main residence, choosing the place not, Lady Gregory saw, because of the ease with which it could be visited by the muses. Rather, he chose it for its proximity to streets where women of circumstance shopped and because of its position in a shadowy side street. Thus no one would notice a respectable woman who was not his wife arriving or leaving in the mornings or the afternoons; no one would hear her cry out as she lay in bed with him; no one would ever know that each time in the hour or so she spent with him she realized that nothing would be enough for her, that she had not merely visited the temple as a tourist might, but she had come to believe in and deeply need the sweet doctrine preached in its warm and exciting confines.

She never once dreamed of being caught. Sir William was often busy in the day; he enjoyed having a long lunch with old associates, or a meeting of some sort about the National Gallery or some political or financial matter. It seemed to please him that his wife went to the shops or to visit her friends during the day as long as she was free in the evenings to accompany him to dinners. He was usually distant, quite distracted. It was, she thought, like being a member of the cabinet with her own tasks and responsibilities with her husband as Prime Minister, happy that he had appointed her, and pleased, it seemed, that she carried out her tasks with the minimum of fuss.

Soon, however, when they were back in England a few months she began to dream, not of his accusing her, or finding her out in the fact, but of what would happen later. She dreamed, for example, that she had been sent home to her parents' house in Roxborough and she was destined to spend her days wandering the corridors of the upper floor, a silent, invisible, ghostly presence. Her mother passed her and did not speak to her. Her sisters came and went but did not seem even to see her. The servants brushed by her. Sometimes, she went downstairs, but there was no chair for her at the dining table and no place for her to sit in the drawing room. Every place had been filled by her sisters and her brothers and their guests and they were all chattering loudly and laughing and being served tea and, no matter how close she came to them, they paid her no attention. They spoke as though she were not there.

The dream changed sometimes. She was in her own house in London or in Coole with her husband and with Robert and their servants but no one saw her, they let her wander in and out of rooms, forlorn, silent, desperate. Her son seemed blind to her as he came towards her. Her husband undressed in their room at night as though she were not there and turned out the lamp in their room while she was still standing at the foot of the bed fully dressed. No one seemed to mind that she haunted the spaces they inhabited because no one noticed her. She had become, in these dreams, invisible to the world.

Despite Sir William's absence from the house during the day and his indifference to how she spent her time as long as she did not cost him too much money, she knew that she could be unlucky. Being found out could come because a friend or an acquaintance or, indeed, an enemy could suspect her and follow her, or Lady Anne could find a key to the room and come with urgent news for her husband or visit suddenly out of sheer curiosity. Blunt was cautious and dependable, she knew, but he was also passionate and excitable. In some fit of rage, or moment where he lost his composure, he could easily, she thought, say enough to someone that they would understand that he was having an affair with the young wife of Sir William Gregory. Her husband had many old friends in London. A note left at his club would be enough to cause him to have her watched and followed. The affair with Blunt, she realized, could not last. As months went by, she left it to Blunt to decide when it should end. It would be best, she thought, if he tired of her and found another. It would be easier to be jealous of someone else than to feel that she had denied herself this deep, fulfilling pleasure for no reason other than fear or caution.

Up to this time she had put no deep thought into what marriage meant. It was, she had vaguely thought, a contract or even a sacrament. It was what happened. It was part of the way things were ordered. Sometimes now, however, when she saw the Blunts socially, or when she read a poem by him or heard someone mention his name, the fact that it was not known and publicly understood that she was with him hurt her deeply, made her experience what existed between them as a kind of emptiness or absence. She knew that if her secret were known or told, it would destroy her life. But as time passed its not being known by anyone at all made her imagine with relish and energy what it would be like to be married to Wilfred Scawen Blunt, to enter a room with him, to leave in a carriage with him, to have her name openly linked with his. It would mean everything. Instead, the time she spent alone with him often came to seem like nothing when it was over. Memory, which was once so sharp and precious for her, came to seem like a dark room in which she wandered longing for the light to be switched on or the curtains pulled back. She longed for the light of publicity, for her secret life to become common knowledge. It was something, she was well aware, that would not happen as long as she lived if she could help it. She would take her pleasure in darkness.

When the affair ended, she felt at times as though it had not happened. There was nothing solid or sure about it. Most women, she thought, had a close, discreet friend to whom such things could be disclosed. She did not. In France, she understood, they had a way of making such things subtly known. Now she understood why. She was lonely without Blunt, but she was lonelier at the idea that the world went on as though she had not loved him. Time would pass and their actions and feelings would seem like a shadow of actions and feelings, but less than a shadow in fact, because cast by something which now seemed to have no real substance.

Thus she wrote the sonnets, using the time she now had to work on rhyme schemes and poetic forms. She wrote in secret about her secret love for him and then kept the paper on which she had written it down:

Where is the pride for which I once was blamed,
My vanity which held its head so high?
. . .
Who would now guess them, as I kiss the ground
On which the feet of him I love have trod,
And bow before his voice whose least sweet sound
Speaks louder to me than the voice of God.

She wrote about her shame, the shame of disclosure, as she disclosed this shame in ink and folded the paper so the next day she could return to read of what she had done and what it meant:

Should ever the day come when this drear world
Shall read the secret which so close I hold,
Should taunts and jeers at my bowed head be hurled,
And all my love and all my shame be told,
I could not, as some doughtier women do,
Fling jests and gold and live the scandal down.

When she asked, some months after their separation, to meet him one more time, his tone in reply was cold, almost brusque. She wondered if he believed that she was going to appeal to him to resume their affair or that she was going to remonstrate with him in some way. She enjoyed how surprised he seemed that she was merely handing him a sheaf of sonnets, making clear as soon as she gave him the pages that she had written them herself. She watched him reading them.

"What shall we do with them?" he asked when he had finished.

"You shall publish them in your next book as though they were written by you," she said.

"But it is clear from the style that they are not."

"Let the world believe that you changed your style for the purposes of writing them. Let your readers believe that you were writing in another voice. That will explain the awkwardness."

"There is no awkwardness. They are very good."

"Then publish them. They are yours."

He agreed then to publish them under his own name in his next book, having made some minor alterations to them. They came out six weeks before Sir William died. Lady Gregory did her husband the favor in those weeks of not keeping the book by her bed but in her study; she managed also to keep these poems out of her mind as she watched over him.

As his widow, she knew who she was and what she had inherited. She had loved him in her way and often missed him. She knew what words like "loved" and "missed" meant when she thought of her husband. When she thought of Blunt on the other hand, she was unsure what anything meant except the sonnets she had written about their love affair. She read them sparingly, often needing them if she woke in the night, but keeping them away from her much of the time. It was enough for her that all over London, in the houses of people who acquired new books of poetry, these poems rested silently and mysterious between the pages. She found solace in the idea that people would read them without knowing their source.

She rebuilt her life as a widow and took care of her son and began, after a suitable period of mourning, to go out in London again and meet people and take part in things. She often wondered if there was someone in the room, or in the street, who had read her sonnets and been puzzled or pained by them, even for a second.

She had read Henry James as his books appeared. In fact, it was a discussion over *Roderick Hudson* that caused Sir William to pay attention to her first. She had read an extract from it but did not have the book. He arranged for it to be sent to her. Once she was married, and visiting Rome with Sir William soon after her marriage, she met James and remembered him fondly as a man who would pay close attention to a woman, even someone as young and provincial as she was, and take her seriously. She remembered asking him at that first meeting in Rome how he could possibly have allowed Isabel Archer to marry the odious Osmond. He told her that Isabel was bound to do something foolish and, if she had not, there would have been no story. And he had enjoyed, he had said, as a poor man himself, bestowing so much money on his heroine. Henry James was kind and witty, she had felt then, and somehow managed not to be glib or patronizing.

Since her husband's death she had seen Henry James a number of times, noticing always how much of himself he held back, how the keenness of his gaze seemed to disguise as much as it disclosed. He had always been very polite to her, and they had often discussed the fate of the orphan Paul Harvey with whose mother they had both been friends. She was surprised one evening to see the novelist at a supper that Lady Layard had taken her to; there were diplomats present and some foreigners, and a few military men and some minor politicians. It was not Henry James's world, and it was Lady Gregory's world only in that an extra woman was needed, as people might need an extra carriage or an extra towel in the bathroom. It did not matter who she was as long as she arrived on time and left at an appropriate moment and did not talk too loudly or compete in any way with the hostess.

It made sense to place her beside Henry James. In the company on a night when politics would be discussed between the men and silliness between the women, neither of them mattered. In a way, she looked forward to having the novelist on her right. Once she disposed of a young Spanish diplomat on her left, she would attend to James and ask him about his work and listen to him with care. When they were all dead, she thought, he would be the one whose name would live on, but it seemed important for those who were rich or powerful to spend their evenings keeping this poor thought at bay.

It was the Spaniard's fingers she noticed, they were long and slender with beautiful rounded nails. She found herself glancing down at them as often as she could, hoping that the diplomat, whose accent was beyond her, would not spot what she was doing. She looked at his eyes and nodded as he spoke, all the time wondering if it would be rude were she to glance down again, this time for longer. Somewhere near London, Wilfred Scawen Blunt was dining too, she thought, perhaps with his wife and some friends. She pictured him reaching for something at the table, a jug of water perhaps and pouring it. She pictured his long slender fingers, the rounded nails, and then began to imagine his hair, how silky it was to the touch and the fine bones of his face and his teeth and his breath.

She stopped herself now and began to concentrate hard on what the Spaniard was saying. She asked him a question which he failed to understand so she repeated it, making it simpler. She asked a number of other questions and listened attentively to the replies. She was relieved when she knew that her time with him was up and she could turn now to Henry James, who seemed heavier than before as though his large head was filled with oak or ivory. As they began to talk, he took her in with his grey eyes, which had a level of pure understanding in them which was almost affecting. For a split second she was tempted to tell him what had happened with Blunt, make it out that it occurred to a friend of hers while visiting Egypt, a friend married to an older man who was seduced by a friend of his, a poet. But she knew it was ridiculous, James would see through her immediately.

Yet something had stirred in her, some sharp need that she had ruminated on in the past but kept out of her mind for some time now. She wanted to say Blunt's name and wondered if she could find a way to ask James if he read his work or admired it. But James was busy describing the best way to see old Rome now that Rome had changed so much and the best way to avoid Americans in Rome, Americans one did not want to see or be associated with. How odd he would think her were she to interrupt him or wait for a break in the conversation and ask him what he thought of the work of Wilfred Scawen Blunt! It was possible he did not even read modern poetry. It would be hard, she thought, to turn the conversation around to Blunt or even find a way to mention him in passing. In any case, James had moved his arena of concern to Venice and was discussing whether it was best to lodge with friends there or find one's own lodging and thus win greater independence.

As he pondered the relative merits of various American hostesses in Venice, going over the quality of their table, the size of their guest rooms, what they put at one's disposal, she thought of love. James sighed and mentioned how a warm personality, especially of the American sort, had a way of cooling one's appreciation of ancient beauty, irrespective of how grand the palazzo this personality was in possession of, indeed irrespective of how fine or fast-moving her gondola.

When he had finished, Lady Gregory turned towards him quietly and asked him if he was tired of people telling him stories he might use in his fiction, or if he viewed such offerings as an essential element in his art. He told her in reply that he always paid attention to what was said to him, and sometimes the germ of a story had come to him from a most unlikely source, and other times, of course, from a most likely and welcome one. He liked to imagine his characters, he said, but he also liked that they might have lived already, to some small extent perhaps, before he painted a new background for them and created a new scenario. Life, he said, life, that was the material that he used and needed. There could never be enough life. But it was only the beginning of course, because life was thin.

There was an eminent London man, she began as James listened, a clergyman known to dine at the best tables, a man of great experience who had many friends, friends who were both surprised and delighted when this man finally married. The lady in question was known to be deeply respectable. But on the day of their wedding as they crossed to France from Dover to Calais, he found a note addressed to her from a man who had clearly been her lover and now felt free, despite her new circumstances, to address her ardently and intimately.

James listened carefully as though he was noting every word. Lady Gregory found that she was trembling and had to control herself; she realized that she would have to speak softly and slowly. She stopped and took a sip of water knowing that if she did not continue in a tone which was easy and nonchalant she would end by giving more away than she wished to give. The clergyman, she went on, was deeply shocked, and, since he had been married merely a few hours to this woman, he decided that, when they had arrived in Paris, he would send her back home to her family, make her an outcast; she would be his wife merely in name. He would not see her again and if her family saw her then it would merely be to take a dim view of her. Instead, however, Lady Gregory went on, when they had arrived at their hotel in Paris the clergyman decided against this action. He informed his errant wife, his piece of damaged goods, that he would keep her, but he would not touch her. He would take her into his house to live, but not as his wife.

Lady Gregory tried to smile casually as she came to the end of the story. She was pleased that her listener had guessed nothing. It was merely a story with a core, a mixture of the French and the English, something that James would understand as being rather particularly his realm. He thanked her and said that he would note the story once he reached his study that evening and he would, he hoped, do justice to it in the note. It was always impossible to know, he added, why one small spark caused a large fire and why another seemed to extinguish itself before it had even flared.

She realized as supper came to an end that she had said as much as she could say, which was, on reflection, she realized, hardly anything at all. She almost wished she had added more detail, that she had told James that the letter came from a poet perhaps, or it contained a set of sonnets whose subject was unmistakable, or that the wife of the clergyman was more than thirty years his junior, or that he was not a clergyman at all, but a former member of parliament and someone who had once held high office. Or that the events in question had happened in Egypt and not on the way to Paris. Or that the woman had never, in fact, been caught, she had been careful and had outlived the husband to whom she had been unfaithful. That she had merely dreamed of and feared being sent home by him or kept apart, never touched.

The next time, she thought, if she found herself seated beside a novelist she would slip in one of these details. She understood perfectly why the idea excited her so much. As Henry James stood up from the table, it gave her a strange sense of satisfaction that she had lodged her secret with him, a secret over-wrapped perhaps, but at least the rudiments of its shape apparent, if not to him then to her for whom these matters were pressing, urgent, and gave meaning to her life. That she had kept the secret and told a small bit of it all at the same time made her feel light as she went to join the ladies for light conversation. It had been, on the whole, she thought, an unexpectedly interesting evening.

WORKS BY HENRY JAMES

CN   *The Complete Notebooks of Henry James.* Ed. Leon Edel and Lyall H. Powers. New York: Oxford UP, 1987.

Fictional works written by Henry James are included as separate entries, without author citation. Works by Tóibín, and others, are included as separate entries with author citations. Fictional characters are entered in the same format as historical figures, that is, last names first.

Colm Tóibín's fiction includes *The South* (1990), *The Heather Blazing* (1992), *The Story of the Night* (1996), *The Blackwater Lightship* (1999), *The Master* (2004), and *Mothers and Sons* (2006). He began his professional writing career in the 1980s as a journalist and editor at venues including *In Dublin*, *Hibernia*, and *Magill*, and continues to work as a reviewer and critic for the *London Review of Books* and the *New York Review of Books*. Tóibín's critical writings have also been published in book form, most prominently *Love in a Dark Time: And Other Exploration of Gay Lives and Literature* (2001), and he has edited anthologies, including the *Penguin Book of Irish Fiction* (1999). Among his nonfiction and travel writings are *Walking Along the Border* (1987), *The Trial of the Generals* (1990), *Homage to Barcelona* (1990), *The Sign of the Cross: Travels in Catholic Europe* (1994), and *The Irish Famine* (1999). *The Master*, a novel that takes Henry James as its subject, was published in 2004 to great critical acclaim. His most recent novel is *Brooklyn* (2009). He has been a Visiting Writer at Stanford University and the University of Texas at Austin. He is now Leonard Milberg Lecturer in Irish Letters at Princeton University.